THE ARCHAEOLOGY OF THE CARIBBEAN

The Archaeology of the Caribbean is a comprehensive synthesis of Caribbean prehistory from the earliest settlement by humans more than 6,000 years ago to the time of European conquest of the islands, from the fifteenth through seventeenth centuries. Samuel Wilson reviews the evidence for migration and cultural change throughout the archipelago, dealing in particular with periods of cultural interaction when groups with different cultures and histories were in contact. He also examines the evolving relationship of the Caribbean people with their environment, as they developed increasingly productive economic systems over time, as well as the emergence of increasingly complex social and political systems, particularly in the Greater Antilles in the centuries before the European conquest. *The Archaeology of the Caribbean* also provides a review of the history of Caribbean archaeology and the individual scholars and ideas that have shaped the field.

Samuel M. Wilson is professor and chairman of the department of anthropology at the University of Texas, Austin. He is the author of several books, including most recently *The Prehistory of Nevis*, and editor of *The Indigenous People of the Caribbean*.

CAMBRIDGE WORLD ARCHAEOLOGY

SERIES EDITOR
NORMAN YOFFEE, *University of Michigan*

EDITORIAL BOARD
SUSAN ALCOCK, *University of Michigan*
TOM DILLEHAY, *University of Kentucky*
STEPHEN SHENNAN, *University College, London*
CARLA SINOPOLI, *University of Michigan*

The *Cambridge World Archaeology* series is addressed to students and professional archaeologists, and to academics in related disciplines. Most volumes present a survey of the archaeology of a region of the world, providing an up-to-date account of research and integrating recent findings with new concerns of interpretation. While the focus is on a specific region, broader cultural trends are discussed and the implications of regional findings for cross-cultural interpretations considered. The authors also bring anthropological and historical expertise to bear on archaeological problems and show how both new data and changing intellectual trends in archaeology shape inferences about the past. More recently, the series has expanded to include thematic volumes.

BOOKS IN THE SERIES

CAMBRIDGE WORLD ARCHAEOLOGY

THE ARCHAEOLOGY OF THE CARIBBEAN

SAMUEL M. WILSON

University of Texas

CAMBRIDGE
UNIVERSITY PRESS

CAMBRIDGE UNIVERSITY PRESS

Cambridge, New York, Melbourne, Madrid, Cape Town, Singapore, São Paulo, Delhi

Cambridge University Press
32 Avenue of the Americas, New York, NY 10013-2473, USA

www.cambridge.org
Information on this title: www.cambridge.org/9780521623339

First published 2007

Printed in the United States of America

A catalog record for this publication is available from the British Library.

Library of Congress Cataloging in Publication Data

Wilson, Samuel Meredith, 1957–
The archaeology of the Caribbean / Samuel M. Wilson.
    p.   cm. – (Cambridge world archaeology)
Includes bibliographical references and index.
ISBN-13: 978-0-521-62333-9 (hardback)
ISBN-10: 0-521-62333-2 (hardback)
ISBN-13: 978-0-521-62622-4 (pbk.)
ISBN-10: 0-521-62622-6 (pbk.)
1. Paleo-Indians – Caribbean Area.   2. Saladoid culture – Caribbean Area.
3. Indians of the West Indies – Colonization.   4. Indians of the West Indies –
First contact with Europeans.   5. Indians of the West Indies – Antiquities.
6. Caribbean Area – Antiquities.   I. Title.   II. Series.
F1619.W55   2007
972.9′01 – dc22   2006101934

ISBN   978-0-521-62333-9 hardback
ISBN   978-0-521-62622-4 paperback

This book is dedicated to the next generation of Caribbeanist scholars,
with thanks to the previous generation.

CONTENTS

LIST OF FIGURES AND TABLE

TABLE

ACKNOWLEDGMENTS

Like most fields, Caribbean archaeology is one in which we learn most of what we know from our colleagues. I certainly learned most of what I know of this region from my friends and fellow researchers in the Caribbean and from the publications of earlier scholars. This learning process was greatly facilitated by the International Association of Caribbean Archaeologists. They have provided an essential forum for communication in their biannual meetings and in their *Proceedings* series, and this has had a profound and positive effect on the field. I acknowledge my great debt to this organization and to all of its members.

I also acknowledge some of those who have had a special impact on me and on the field as a whole. I began with the idea of separating the following into generations or cohorts of scholars but came to realize I would offend too many people by misclassifying them with their younger or older colleagues. In any case, I am greatly indebted to the following friends and colleagues, with apologies to those I have failed to include: Ricardo Alegría; Louis Allaire; Andrzej and Magdalena Antczak; Manuel García Arevalo; Doug Armstrong; Mary Jane Berman; Berard Benoît; Margaret Bradford; Betsy Carlson; Luis Chanlatte Baik; Michael Cinquino; John Crock; Alissandra Cummins; Antonio Curet; Dave Davis; Kathy Deagan; André and Claude Delpuech; Lourdes Dominguez; Peter Drewett; Star Farr; Jorge Febles; Lyle and Eleanor Gittens; Pedro Godo; Mary Hill Harris; Peter Harris; Jay Haviser; Michele Hayward; Corinne

Hofman; Menno Hoogland; Quetta Kaye; Sebastian Knippenberg; Diana López; Fernando Luna Calderon; Emily Lundberg; Shirley McGinnis; Marisol Meléndez; Birgit Faber Morse; Reg Murphy; Yvonne Narganes; Lee Newsom; Desmond and Lisa Nicholson; José Oliver; Elpidio Ortega; Pepe Ortíz; Gus Pantel; Jim Peterson; Henri, Hugues, and Bernard Petitjean Roget; Holly Righter; Virginia Rivera; Dave and Joan Robinson; Miguel Rodríguez; Reniel Rodríguez; Peter Roe; Dan Rogers; Anna Roosevelt; Stephen Rostain; Nathalie Serrand; Peter Siegel; Anne Stokes; Jalil Sued Badillo; Lesley Sutty; Glenis Tavarez; Dicey Taylor; Bernardo Vega; Aad Versteeg; Jeff Walker; David Watters; Ken Wild; Liz Wing; John Winter; and Alberta Zucci.

I must offer special thanks to Arie Boomert, Antonio Curet, Bill Keegan, José Oliver, Estrella Rey, Ben Rouse, and Marcio Veloz Maggiolo for their general influence on my thinking about these matters and for help with this project specifically. And, as always, my love and thanks to Cory, Nellie, and Marshall.

CHAPTER I

INTRODUCTION

Nearly 6,000 years ago, people took the bold step of paddling their canoes out beyond the horizon of the Caribbean Sea, where no land could be seen. They were well rewarded for taking this risk, for they found a large, rich, and uninhabited chain of islands that stretched 1,500 km and contained more than 200,000 sq km of land. It was the last large area of the Americas to be explored and populated. These discoverers and their descendants have lived in the Caribbean ever since. They were eventually joined by people from other parts of the Americas and from Europe, Africa, and Asia. In the millennia that followed, their descendants went through a series of changes that in some ways paralleled what happened with people in other parts of the Americas: they developed an efficient economy that worked well in the island setting and eventually adopted a sedentary, horticultural way of life based in part on domesticated plants brought from South America.

But ever since people first moved into the Caribbean they have followed a distinctive course, one that differs from the rest of the Americas despite nearly constant contacts between Caribbean people and the surrounding mainlands. These first colonists refashioned the island environments, unintentionally and intentionally, to suit their purposes, just as present-day Caribbean people are doing. They brought in many new species and caused the extinction of many others. Through time they grew to be diversified into many distinctive regional groups, creating a mosaic of cultures across the islands.

Throughout its history, the indigenous people of the Lesser Antilles developed and redeveloped interisland networks for trade and other kinds of interaction. They also maintained connections with the South American mainland that lasted well into colonial times. In the last centuries before contact, large and complex polities emerged in the Greater Antilles. They had enduring hierarchies of social status and large political units organizing tens of thousands of people. When Columbus and his company arrived in 1492, they witnessed large and dense populations living in villages of up to several thousand people. These complex societies were supported by intensive agriculture and other kinds of specialized production and the distribution of food, salt, stone, and other raw materials. Scholars have come to call these people the Taíno, borrowing one of the many names they had for themselves (Rouse 1992).

The island people of the Greater Antilles bore the brunt of the first wave of European conquest in the New World. Taíno society quickly disintegrated after the arrival of the first European explorers (Anderson-Córdova 1990; Deagan 1995; Sauer 1966; Wilson 1990). The spread of epidemic diseases took the highest toll, but Spanish tribute and labor demands also undermined the complexly integrated Taíno economy, causing famine to spread through the Greater Antilles. The Bahamas were also badly affected by disease and by the removal of people who were enslaved and taken to Hispaniola (now the Dominican Republic and Haiti) to serve as forced labor (Keegan 1992).

The indigenous people of the Lesser Antilles fared slightly better in the century after European contact, principally because they were able to survive the influx of European diseases more successfully (Hulme 1986; Wilson 1997). They typically lived in smaller villages and were more mobile. Although they also suffered from disease and raids, they could take to their canoes and flee Europeans who might attack or attempt to enslave them. These Lesser Antillean people, who came be known as the Island Caribs, tenaciously fought European attempts to colonize their islands for nearly two centuries, eventually making peace and living in reserved areas on a few of the islands or in Central America (Allaire 1997; Gonzalez 1988).

Since the time of Charles Darwin's travels in the nineteenth century, there has been a temptation to think of islands as "laboratories" for the study of biological or cultural processes – isolated places where changes could take place over long spans of time, unaffected by the outside world. Darwin saw the Galapagos Islands as a natural laboratory within which he could study evolution by means of natural selection. It would be very misleading to approach the Caribbean islands in such a way, however, for in terms of their human history they were certainly not isolated places. From the earliest human colonization, the islands were linked to one another by the sea, not separated by it. Nevertheless, islands have special properties with implications for their human occupation (Renfrew and Wagstaff 1982). Islands in general, and the Caribbean islands in particular, are fascinating places to research the interaction of people with the environment, as well as the complex interplay of geography and culture. Cyprian Broodbank (2000:3), writing about the Aegean in *An Island Archaeology of the Early Cyclades*, advocates the development of an archaeological approach specifically developed for island environments, an approach that

> . . . encourages a structure of enquiry centred around a series of key questions about people on islands that are common to island archaeology all over the world. Why did people go to islands? How did they choose to live after arrival? How were people's lives shaped by, and how did they reshape, in physical but also cognitive terms, the islands that they inhabited? What kinds of interaction took place between island communities, and also between islanders and other, non-insular communities? How did external contacts affect the cultures of islanders? How and why did island societies 'end' – if indeed they did?

All of these questions are relevant to the present study and help to call attention to some of the distinctive characteristics of Caribbean history. In considering what makes the Caribbean such a unique historical situation, it is important to recognize that the colonization of the Antilles took place long after the rest of the Americas was well explored and occupied. At around 4000 B.C. the islands were something of a "last frontier" – a large, rich, and uninhabited part of the hemisphere. The islands had escaped colonization for so long

because the first long step out to the archipelago was such a difficult one. The places where the Caribbean islands are closest to the
mainland are western Cuba, Trinidad and Tobago, and the northern
Bahamas. It is nearly 200 km from the Yucatan peninsula out to the
western tip of Cuba, and on the other end of the archipelago there
is a 125-km gap between Tobago and Grenada (Figure 1.1). It is
about 100 km from Florida out to the nearest of the Bahamas. Once
past the first step, however, the other passages are relatively easy. For
example, in the southern Lesser Antilles, after the first passage of
125 km, the next island in the chain is in sight or otherwise apparent,
all the way to Cuba. In historical times interisland contact via canoes
was common, and this was probably true from the very beginnings of
the human colonization of the Caribbean (Watters and Rouse 1989).

THEMES EXPLORED IN THIS SURVEY

This volume aims to provide a synthetic overview of what is known
of the prehistory and early colonial history of the indigenous people
of the Caribbean. Several themes receive special emphasis. First, it
is apparent that the Caribbean had a great degree of cultural diversity even in prehistory. Today it is clear that the islands are culturally and linguistically diverse, divided as they are among speakers
of Spanish, French, Dutch, English, Hindi, Papiamento, and many
distinct Creole languages. But traditional views of the precontact
Caribbean, based in part on mistaken ethnohistoric perspectives, had
divided the archipelago between only two large and relatively homogeneous groups: the Arawaks and the Caribs. In that view, which
began with Columbus's very imperfect attempts to understand the
cultural situation he encountered, the Island Caribs were "warlike"
recent arrivals from the South American mainland, engaged in con-
quering their way up through the Lesser Antilles. In the Greater
Antilles, according to this story, the Arawaks or Taíno lived in their
villages in peace. The story of "peaceful" Arawaks and invading
Caribs is still taught in Caribbean schools and elsewhere.

It now appears that at the time of the Europeans' arrival the
archipelago was much more complicated and diverse than the explorers thought. In fact, the diversity and cultural interaction in the

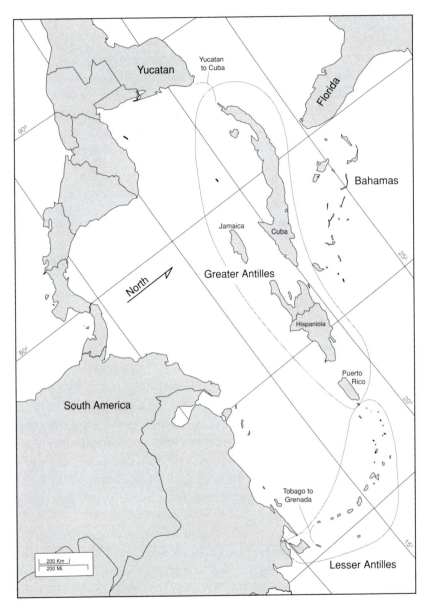

Figure 1.1. Map of the Caribbean.

islands played a critical role in culture change throughout Caribbean prehistory. I will argue that in situations in which people with different ancestries and cultures live in close proximity and interact intensely, an individual or group gains little advantage by the strategy of clinging to old and conservative ways. Instead, invention and innovation is a better strategy for finding new solutions to problems and for attracting followers and allies. In looking at the modern situation, the cultural impact of the Caribbean on the world is far out of proportion to its size. With fewer than 40 million people (in 2003; Rand McNally World Atlas 2004), the entire population of the 30 or so Caribbean countries is less than that of Poland, Tanzania, or Colombia. But the region has disproportionate influence in terms of world music, art, literature, sports, and global cultural trends. I believe the explanation is that in multicultural situations there is more opportunity and indeed a great advantage to combining genres, styles, and ideas in new ways. This seems to have been the case in the prehistoric Caribbean just as it is in the region today.

Tracking cultural diversity in the archaeological record is a difficult matter, however; and it is a focus of research that is being explored at present by many archaeologists. Some distinctive markers of a person's cultural identity can be subtle or displayed in ways that archaeologists cannot recover. For example, patterns of dress, hair styles, tattoos, and other things are not preserved archaeologically. Fortunately for archaeologists, other markers of identity are more obvious and well preserved. The difficulty, as we will see in the discussion of cultural variability in Saladoid times, is in interpreting what these markers and the differences between them really mean.

A second theme, closely intertwined with the first, involves the attempt to understand the factors that led to the emergence of complex societies in the region. By "complex societies," archaeologists generally mean societies that have some or most of the following characteristics: (1) some sort of permanent hierarchy of social statuses that are determined by birth more than achievement; (2) a demographic scale or size to support nonproducing elites, usually 10,000 people or more; and (3) a system of political organization that involves decision making at above the village or community level (Curet [2003] provides a good discussion of the concept of complex or middle-range societies in the Caribbean). These characteristics emerged in parts of the Caribbean between A.D. 500 and the time of European conquest, and so for archaeologists interested in how this process takes place, this has been an important topic of investigation. An important aspect of the Caribbean case is that the emergence of complex society is relatively recent, compared to the first time it happened, in Mesopotamia more than 6,000 years ago. Another important parameter is that these social and political changes occurred in relative isolation from other more powerful polities. It is reasonably clear that complex Caribbean polities emerged for internal reasons, not because of external pressures.

Just what range of factors were involved in the emergence of complex societies in the Caribbean is not completely clear, but they likely include such things as changes in the economic basis of society, population growth, changing connections with groups both inside and outside the Caribbean, control of trade and knowledge, competition for resources, and strategies for dealing with internal and external threats. The theme of complex society emergence is particularly important in Chapter 3, which deals with the Saladoid phenomena and again in Chapters 4 and 5 dealing with the Taíno.

Another theme of this volume is that interisland networks were very important throughout time, particularly in the Lesser Antilles and Bahamas. Evidence is beginning to emerge for shifting alliances of people from different islands, who certainly traded and probably also intermarried and allied with one another for raiding or defense (Delpuech and Hofman 2004). These interisland networks expanded the horizons of the participants' social world, but more importantly the economic and alliance networks made the occupation of the islands and island groups possible. As will be discussed, in later prehistory the breakdown of some of these networks preceded and probably precipitated the abandonment of several adjacent islands (Crock and Petersen 2004; Hofman and Hoogland 2004; and other papers in Delpuech and Hofman 2004). Keegan and others have also discussed interactions among the Bahamian islands and between them and the Greater Antilles (Keegan 1992). Both of these cases suggest that it is important not to think of islands as isolates; rather, populations from several islands were likely linked in networks of interaction (Rouse 1986).

A final theme that is given special attention is the importance of long-distance interaction, especially with people outside the Caribbean. We know there was sustained contact between the Lesser Antilles and the South American mainland and have some evidence for contact between the Greater Antilles and Central America, and perhaps the Bahamas and North America as well. But these types of data are elusive and difficult to use with confidence if it involves artifacts that did not come from well-documented contexts. As discussed in later sections of the book, it seems increasingly likely that long-distance interactions and contacts with other regions may have played a significant role in the course of Caribbean prehistory.

ENVIRONMENTAL CONSIDERATIONS

The strategy taken in this volume is not to attempt to "set the environmental stage" on which a human drama is played, because environmental change is itself such an important part of that story. Instead, the strategy is to address human–environmental interactions period by period, as they occurred. Nevertheless, it is necessary to make a few general points about Caribbean environments and the opportunities they provide and the constraints they impose. It is also possible to make some observations about the perceptions about tropical environments that foreign researchers have brought with them to the Caribbean.

First and perhaps most important, all the islands of the Caribbean are very different from one another. They vary widely on a number of axes – size, topography, climate, environmental richness, and diversity, to name a few.

A very important difference among the islands is their size. When one travels through the archipelago the differences are obvious, but their magnitude is hard to gauge. The islands of the Greater Antilles are enormous compared to the Lesser Antilles (Figure 1.1). The largest island, Cuba, is nearly 10 times larger than all of the Lesser Antilles combined. All together, the Lesser Antilles comprise about 12,000 sq km, whereas the combined Greater Antilles total about

Figure 1.2. View of the volcanic cone of the island of Nevis from the west.

194,000 sq km. These differences in size have significant implications for the inhabitants' economy, social and political organization, and demography. In the Lesser Antilles, people's diets were almost always linked to ocean resources, whereas in the interior of the large islands people often had a wholly terrestrial food supply. Productive resources such as the large and fertile valleys of the Greater Antilles are rare on most of the Lesser Antilles. The larger islands clearly support larger populations in proportion to their size, but they also may have supported higher population densities due to the general productivity of the land, especially the large interior valleys. Groups inhabiting the same island did not necessarily interact more than those on adjacent islands, however, and in some cases they may have been more isolated due to geographic barriers, for example, mountain ranges or the distances between valleys.

The topography of the Caribbean islands is also very diverse, reflecting the differing underlying geology. A tectonic plate boundary between the expanding Atlantic plate and the Caribbean plate accounts for the volcanism and uplift of the arc of the Lesser Antilles. The collision of these two plates has produced two very different kinds of islands in the Lesser Antilles. There are volcanic islands that have been raised up by an arc of eruptions stretching from Grenada, off the coast of South America, up to the island of Saba almost 1,000 km up the archipelago (Figures 1.2 and 1.3 show the volcanic cone of the island of Nevis in the Leeward Islands). This "ring of fire" is still active, as the 1995 eruption on Montserrat demonstrates. As my colleagues and I were carrying out excavations on the east coast of Nevis in the late 1990s we saw the incessant plume of smoke from Montserrat, and the eruption has continued for more than 10 years. The 1902 eruption of Mt. Pelée on Martinique engulfed and destroyed the town of Saint Pierre, and many *soufrieres* and hot springs may be found up and down the arc. The same tectonic phenomenon accounts for the uplift of many islands with sedimentary substrates. These much older geological formations generally appear as relatively flat islands without the pronounced topography of the volcanic isles. The island of Guadeloupe is a good example of both structures because it is really two very different islands that happen to touch. Basse Terre on the western half is a series of volcanoes, the highest of which rises to 1,467 m (it last erupted in 1956). On the eastern side, Grande Terre is made of 20-million-year-old Miocene limestone, some dissected with karstic features, and there are only a few hundred meters of topography in all.

The other major landforms in the Caribbean are the faultblock mountains of the Greater Antilles. These mountains are really continuations of the cordillera systems of Central America. The mountain systems of Guatemala and Belize carry across to the eastern province of Cuba and the northern cordillera of Hispaniola. A southern cordillera extends from Honduras and Nicaragua to become the backbone of Jamaica and the bulk of Hispaniola's Cordillera Central (Blume 1972:27–39). The same range underlies Puerto Rico's central cordillera. Beneath Puerto Rico are primarily uplifted and deformed sedimentary rocks, and in Hispaniola there are also igneous and crystalline complexes (which contained gold and helped make Hispaniola the first target for intensive European colonization in the Americas).

In addition to this structural diversity, there is considerable variability through the archipelago in terms of other environmental variables such as climate, fauna, flora, and off-shore resources. In the Caribbean the interaction between people and the environment has been of enormous importance, arguably more dramatic than in non-island contexts. From their earliest arrival, people had an immense impact on the environment they entered; they caused a host of

Figure 1.3. The central volcano of the island of Nevis, showing overgrazing and erosion near the coast.

extinctions, introduced hundreds of species, and changed the vegetation, hydrology, and even climate of whole islands (Woods and Sergile 2001). Indeed, they significantly altered their environments, and as Broodbank provocatively notes, they may have done so intentionally (Broodbank 2000:7). "It is likely," Broodbank observes, "... that islanders have always been conscious of their role as world-makers in terms of the transformation of their environments."

The scale of environmental change increased during the time of colonial conquest, when entire islands were cleared of their tropical forests for large-scale agricultural production, and this impact continues today with tourism development (Watts 1987). European and African migrants also transformed the Caribbean flora and fauna intentionally, bringing in hosts of new plants and animals. The environments we see at present scarcely resemble those seen by the first migrants.

Climate is a surprisingly important variable in understanding Caribbean environments. For people from more northerly or southerly latitudes the Caribbean climate seems unchanging – perfect year-round. It is easy to miss finer-scale climatic and environmental diversity if one comes from a region with marked seasons in which plants and animals go dormant and the earth is covered with

Figure 1.4. The rain forest in El Yunque National Forest, Puerto Rico.

snow. In the tropical Caribbean, nevertheless, seasonal changes are very important, with different kinds of foods available at different times. More important than temperature variation is the fact that rains are seasonal. There is a dry season from December to May and a wet season from June to November (Blume 1972). Annual precipitation varies greatly depending on altitude and whether one is on the windward or leeward side of an island. Some of the low,

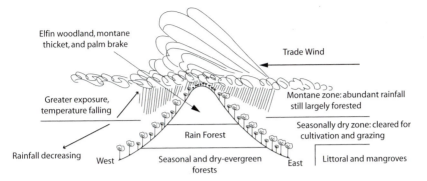

Figure 1.5. John Stewart Beard's (1949) idealized cross section of a Caribbean island.

dry Bahamian islands receive fewer than 750 mm (29 inches) of rainfall annually (Blume 1972:15–26). In El Yunque National Forest in Puerto Rico, however, more than 3,048 mm (120 inches) fall and there are other mountainous areas in the Caribbean that receive even more (Figure 1.4). Figure 1.5 shows John Stewart Beard's (1949) idealized cross section of a Caribbean island, showing how elevation affects ecological zones and generates rainfall.

One thing that has not changed in the Caribbean environment in recent millennia is hurricanes. From the time of the earliest colonizations people would have experienced these devastating storms, and it is reflected in the indigenous cosmology, calendar, and architecture. The word *hurricane* itself comes from the Taíno word *huracán* (Highfield 1997). In trying to understand the importance of the seasons, storms, and the related calendrical and cosmological features of prehistoric Caribbean cultures, one may see several parallels with Polynesia. In both areas the season of storms is carefully marked and mythologically significant. There are other interesting ideographic parallels between Polynesia and the Caribbean: to name just one, in both areas sea creatures, birds, and powerful humans or human spirits become more and more important through time and take the place of mainland animals in the islanders' iconography (Kirch 1984; McGinnis 1997).

Another important environmental issue for understanding the human history of the region is the physical layout of the archipelago.

It is in a sense linear – a long chain of small and large islands stretching 2,500 km from South America to Florida and the Yucatán. This physical pattern is a significant factor in understanding such things as the development of trade and interaction spheres, as well as the process of ethnic/cultural divergence. As Watters and Rouse (1989) pointed out, people who did not grow up in the islands tend to think of each island as isolated, surrounded by the barrier of the sea. To canoe-borne people who spent a lot of time on the water, the straits between islands were connections, not barriers. It was often easier to make use of the facing coast of the next island in the series than it was to use the opposite side of one's own island, and trade, as well as social and political alliances in the prehistoric Caribbean, reflect that.

As noted earlier, the difference in the sizes of the Greater and Lesser Antilles is profound, with the surface area of the Greater Antilles 16 times greater than that of the Lesser Antilles. In the Lesser Antilles, inhabitants from the time of the earliest migrants required interisland mobility to survive. They needed to travel to have access to particular kinds of raw materials; for example, there is one chert (or flint) source on Antigua that was used by people many hundreds of kilometers up and down the archipelago consistently through time (Knippenberg 1999a). Probably much more important than access to raw materials, people had to travel to keep in touch with a wider social network – to trade, share knowledge, intermarry, and maintain a shared language and cultural identity. In the Greater Antilles interisland travel was never abandoned, but it was less essential to survival. At times, a big island could itself be seen as comparable to a group of islands, with relatively isolated groups divided by cordilleras or occupying remote river drainages. At the time of European contact, there was considerable cultural diversity within the Greater Antilles, even on a single island (Wilson 1993).

As noted earlier, the large islands had large river valleys, a kind of terrain that was rare or nonexistent in the Lesser Antilles. These were the sites of some of the densest populations in the Caribbean. The largest was the central valley of Hispaniola drained by the Yaqui del Norte and the Yuna Rivers (Figure 1.6). At the time of the conquest, it held several complex polities – probably the largest in

Figure 1.6. The central valley (Vega Real) in the Dominican Republic.

the Caribbean. There are many smaller but comparable valleys on Hispaniola, Cuba, Jamaica, and Puerto Rico.

The Lesser Antilles also possessed productive resources in the form of rich offshore habitats. Some of the shallow shelves and banks surrounding islands are much larger than the islands themselves, suggesting that it is deceptive to use an island's size as a measure of its productive potential. The accessibility of offshore resources of course depended on the technology and knowledge used to exploit it, which, as we shall see, improved gradually through the centuries and millennia of the occupation of the Lesser Antilles.

ON THE DEVELOPMENT OF CARIBBEAN ARCHAEOLOGY

At the beginning of the twenty-first century, Caribbean archaeology is in a period of transition. In the previous century, much of the archaeological emphasis was on refining artifact chronologies, understanding migrations of peoples, and, to an extent, reconstructing economic strategies (see Keegan 2000 for a review). A general outline of archaeological chronology in the Caribbean is now fairly complete, at least in broad strokes. Of course, many islands and areas are still relatively unknown, and a focus on basic culture history will be important in Caribbean archaeology for a long time to come.

In many areas, however, scholars are attempting to shift attention to processes of cultural change and other issues (Benoît and Vidal 2001; Boomert 2000; Curet 2005; Delpuech and Hofman 2004). The rise of complex societies is one such process, but others include ethnogenesis, which accounts for the region's ethnic heterogeneity and cultural synthesis, or "acculturation," which occurred many times in the Caribbean (Agorsah 1995; Whitehead 1988; Wilson 1993). Others are carrying out detailed research at the household level, exploring domestic production and social organization and their relationship to other issues such as political centralization (Curet and Oliver 1998; Siegel 1992). Another area of interest is in the long-term change in systems of symbols and meanings that took place when lowland river people moved into the islands: over centuries, they substituted new iconographic motifs for symbolically powerful lowland creatures such as jaguars and caymans (Roe 1989). In prehistory as well as in historic times, we can see Caribbean cultures constantly evolving and changing, reinventing and transforming themselves in a social, political, and environmental context that is itself constantly changing.

One of the most exciting parts of Caribbean archaeology is the degree to which it is an exercise in international communication and cooperation. Archaeologists working in the region come from most of the Caribbean nations, as well as from Canada, Denmark, France, Holland, Spain, the United Kingdom, the United States, Venezuela, and many other Latin American countries. At times, different researchers and groups have pursued very different intellectual projects. Some, for example, attempted to fit Caribbean artifacts and cultures into a system of artifact classification called the Midwestern taxonomic system, whereas other scholars were attempting to find a sequence of Marx's modes of production in their archaeological data. The largest point of common interest has been in the general cultural history of the Caribbean, which no one could reconstruct without access to the work carried out by the others. In the late twentieth century, a great number of individuals were important participants in the process of piecing together the outlines of Caribbean prehistory, including (to name just a few) Ricardo Alegría, Luis Chanlatte Baik, Ripley and Adelaide Bullen, Edgar Clerc, Cayetano Coll y Toste, José Cruxent, Desmond Nicholson, Estrella Rey, Jacques Petitjean Roget, Irving Rouse, Ernesto Tabío, and Marcio Veloz Maggiolo.

Very important in this process of international cooperation are the biennial meetings of the International Association for Caribbean Archaeology (the IACA is alternatively known in French as the Association Internationale d'Archéologie de la Caraïbe or AIAC and in Spanish as the Asociación Internacional de Arqueología del Caribe or AIAC). This remarkable group has been able to share knowledge and produce results that could not be attained by individuals or national groups. That such a high level of cooperation has been possible is even more impressive when one considers the history of international hostility, colonialism, and racism that the Caribbean has experienced and continues to experience. It has not been a happy accident that such good cooperation and camaraderie has been possible – it has required consistent effort by people of good will who struggle to understand and make themselves understood across barriers of language, culture, and historical difference. The generation of archaeologists who began the IACA (then called the Congrès International d'Etudes des Civilisations Précolombiennes des Petites Antilles) at a meeting in Fort-de-France, Martinique, in July 1961 made a tremendous contribution to Caribbean archaeology, and we in subsequent generations should strive to continue this effort.

ON THE BEGINNINGS OF CARIBBEAN ARCHAEOLOGY

There has been speculation about the prehistory of the Caribbean since the explorations of the first European visitors, and there was almost certainly curiosity among the islanders about the tools and remains of their forebears. The early chronicler Bartolomé de Las Casas, writing in the 1500s, is probably the first published Caribbean archaeologist. He said,

> I have seen in these mines of Cibao, a *stadia* or two deep in the virgin earth, in the plains at the foot of some hills, burned wood and ashes as if a few days ago a fire was made there. And for the same reason we have to conclude that in other times the river came near there, and in that place they made a fire, and

afterwards the river went away. The soil brought from the hills by the rains covered it [the fire site]. And because this could not happen except by the passage of many years and most ancient time, there is a great argument that the people of these islands and continent are very ancient. (1951:375)

Many writers in the late 19th and early 20th centuries commented on the archaeological remains of the indigenous people of the Caribbean, and it is clear from these early writings that there was the general sense that several different archaeological cultures had existed in the Caribbean. There was a consensus that these different cultures had flourished at different times and that the sequence of fluorescences was related to their order of migration to the Caribbean. In 1924, Swedish archaeologist Sven Loven published his *Über die Wurzeln der tainischen Kultur* in German; the English translation was published in 1935. His widely shared view was that there were "four distinct races in the West Indies properly speaking, from historical sources. The names are given in the order which they must have immigrated" (1935:2). He then listed (1) Guanahatabeyes, (Siboneyes), (2) Island-Arawaks, (3) Maçoriges (Ciguayos), and (4) Island-Caribs.

Jesse Walter Fewkes, in his analysis of the artifacts in the Heye Collection (Fewkes 1922; see also his 1907 work on Puerto Rico and neighboring islands), had proposed "three cultural epochs, grading into each other, which may indicate a sequence in time or distinct cultural stages. These epochs were of the cave dwellers, the agriculturalists, and the Carib" (Fewkes 1922:56). These three groups corresponded to Loven's groups 1, 2, and 4. Fewkes noted that all three groups were still living in the Caribbean at the time of European conquest. His objective with the analysis of the Heye collection was not so much to establish a chronology but rather to look for geographical areas of cultural similarity, of which he identified several.

An important step came in the 1920s, when Gudmund Hatt, a professor of archaeology at Copenhagen University in Denmark, established a more explicit provisional archaeological sequence for the region. He carried out archaeological research on the island of St. Croix in the early 1920s, excavating about 30 sites in the Virgin

Islands (Morse 1995:473–4). The Virgin Islands had been a Danish possession in the Caribbean until the United States bought the islands in 1917 for $25 million. They nevertheless remained an area of Danish interest thereafter. Although others had excavated in the Caribbean – indeed Theodoor de Booy of the American Museum of Natural History had worked on some of the same sites excavated by Professor Hatt (de Booy 1919) – Hatt carefully analyzed the stratigraphy of the sites he excavated, and based on that evidence he proposed a three-phase sequence for the prehistory of the Virgin Islands (Hatt 1924). He called the first phase Krum Bay, after the preceramic site he explored on the southeast coast of St. Thomas. As discussed in Chapter 2, it was characterized by ground and flaked stone tools, lots of shellfish, and a lack of pottery. Hatt's second phase was Coral Bay–Longford, referring to sites with white-on-red painted pottery and other Saladoid characteristics. The third and most recent phase he called Magens Bay–Salt River. These sites contained somewhat less carefully made pottery vessels with modeling and incision and with no white-on-red painting. The site of the Salt River, on the northern coast of St. Croix, also had a ball court comparable to those at Taíno sites in Puerto Rico and the rest of the Greater Antilles.

DISCUSSION OF CHRONOLOGY, TAXONOMY, AND TERMINOLOGY

The three-period chronological sequence for the Caribbean suggested by these earlier investigators is still essentially intact today, although it has become more complex and better understood. Within the field of Caribbean archaeology as it has developed, there has been considerable variability in how people have interpreted this sequence, and in the names they have given to the phases, as they have variously constructed them. Because this has been a relatively important issue in Caribbean archaeology and an important one for presenting a narrative of Caribbean prehistory, we must briefly explore terminological issues here.

In the years following Hatt's work, the relative chronology he proposed was refined and elaborated on considerably. The work of Irving Rouse in Haiti (1939, 1941b) and Cuba (1942) and the work

supported by the New York Academy of Sciences in Puerto Rico
(Mason 1941; Rainey 1941; Rouse 1941a, 1952) provided a great
deal of new and systematically collected archaeological data. Based
on this and his ongoing research in the 1950s, Rouse proposed a
relative time scale with periods, identified by Roman numerals I
through IV, extending from the earliest human occupation to the
time after the arrival of Europeans (Rouse 1964). These periods were
subsequently subdivided (for example, into periods III-a and III-b)
and refined. Based on the characteristics of the artifacts, Rouse and
others employing his methodology defined "series" grouping complexes and styles. Series were designated by the suffix "–oid" and,
in a refinement suggested by Gary Vescelius (1980), were further
subdivided into subseries, which ended in "–an." Thus, for example, the earliest preceramic assemblages in the Greater Antilles were
called Casimiroid after the site of Casimira, where these artifacts
had first been described. Within this series, a further differentiation was proposed between Cuban sites, of which Cayo Redondo
was the first representative, and Haitian sites, of which Couri was
the first good case. Under the system of series and subseries, the
two subseries came to be called Redondan Casimiroid and Courian
Casimiroid. In Chapter 3 of this volume we discuss the "Saladoid"
phenomena, which refers to a period in which sedentary agriculturalists moved from South America up through the Lesser Antilles
and Puerto Rico. It is named after the Venezuelan site of Saladero
(Cruxent and Rouse 1969).

The series and subseries classification scheme has been criticized
by several scholars (e.g., Keegan 2000; Keegan and Rodríguez 2005).
As Keegan and Rodríguez (2005) note, "the major problem with
this framework comes from an emphasis on similarities. When one
looks only at the distribution of series, the impression is that all of the
different social groups in the Caribbean were members of one culture. . . . " In a 2001 article William Keegan suggested that we should,
"avoid the OID" entirely. I agree that Rouse's method for organizing archaeological variability in a space–time grid does have some
unfortunate consequences for some kinds of interpretation. This
system is weakest in trying to reflect long periods of gradual change
or the diverging developments of groups with a shared ancestry. It is

certainly the case, however, that a lot of the terminology that came out of Rouse's systematic work – Casimiroid, Ostionoid, Saladoid, Chicoid, and so on – has been important in Caribbean archaeology and is deeply entrenched in the literature in the Caribbean. I have kept those designations here because I think it would be needlessly confusing to invent substitutes.

Other systems for describing the chronological and archaeological variability are also in use in Caribbean archaeology. Cuban archaeologists have developed a system of classification based on the economic systems of the prehistoric people. This system was influenced by Tabío and Rey's focus on the relations of production in their 1966 book, *Prehistoria de Cuba*, and developed by subsequent generations of Cuban archaeologists. In 1995 a great deal of information on Cuban archaeology was assembled on the CD-ROM "Taíno: Arqueología de Cuba" by the Centro de Antropología. The work was produced by nearly 40 collaborators and was edited by Jorge Febles (1995). The organizational framework for classifying archaeological remains is widely used in Cuba and elsewhere. It consists of two stages of economic development – the economy of appropriation and the economy of food production – representing the delineation between hunter-gatherers and horticulturalists. Within the economy of appropriation are three phases: hunting, fishing and collecting, and the protoagricultural phase. The economy of food production is dominated by the agricultural phase. Within this overall economic framework, the archaeologists discuss all aspects of life, including social and political organization, language, religion, and art, and all of the technologies represented in the archaeological record. This classification scheme was also critiqued by Keegan and Rodríguez (2005), who argued that, "if the sole purpose of our work is to fit the past to preconceived evolutionary stages, then the past becomes fixed and not a means for understanding."

Another system of classification in a sense combines the two schemes just mentioned. Luis Chanlatte (1995) proposes one major division between an early period called Archaic and a later period of farmer-potters (*arcaicos* and *agroalfareros*). Within the Archaic, Chanlatte defines a preceramic period in which there was little or no interaction with pottery-making groups outside the islands and an aceramic period of development that took place with some inter-action between Archaic and people who made ceramics and prac-ticed horticulture. Within the Agroalfarero or farmer-potter period Chanlatte describes two migrations – Agroalferero I and II – repre-senting separate migrations that in Rouse's scheme would be called Huecoid and Saladoid. From the interaction of these groups and Archaic people emerges the Antillean Formative, which includes all subsequent prehistoric people. Agroalfarero III includes people between about 460 and 1025 A.D., and Agroalfarero IV refers to the late Taíno fluorescence seen by Spanish chroniclers.

It has been difficult for many people interested in Caribbean archaeology to make sense of what seems like a daunting profu-sion of series, phases, styles, periods, subseries, complexes, and other descriptive or taxonomic units. However, it seems like a problem of translation, because Caribbean archaeology is such a polyglot enter-prise. It is actually, however, a more complex issue, because there is no simple way of classifying human cultures in time and space, and the best classificatory scheme depends a great deal on what sorts of questions one is asking. If a scholar is interested in the changing economic strategies of prehistoric people through time, his or her system of classification will likely be based on economic data. If one is interested in the history of cultural groups as they move through a region and change through time, changes in the characteristics of durable artifacts such as pottery or other nonperishable artifacts may take precedence. In fact, however, most scholars are interested in a wide range of phenomena about human societies in the past, and so we have a confusing situation with multiple classificatory schemes, aims, and research directions. José Oliver (1989:212–22) makes a compelling argument that multiple levels of taxonomic resolution are needed: "Each of these classificatory units has been used in response to specific problems, ranging in scope from a single site to an entire country. . . . Undoubtedly, each approach has its merits. However, classification is only useful to the degree that it can help to address or better understand the problems at hand" (1989:314). Oliver pro-posed a hierarchical classificatory model going from macro-tradition to tradition and then subtradition, with complex or style and phase being the lowest taxonomic level (1989:218–19). This seems very reasonable to me, although again I have not tried to recast what we know about Caribbean prehistory in new terms. Here the aim is to describe the scholarly conclusions about Caribbean prehistory in historical context, which has involved maintaining the existing terminology.

ORGANIZATION OF THE VOLUME

The next chapter deals with the earliest colonization of the Antilles, when people crossed the Yucatan Channel from the Central American mainland to Cuba. It deals with the earliest bold movement of people into the islands and discusses the sites they chose to inhabit and the pristine environment they encountered. A second migration occurred more than a millennium later, this one up through the Lesser Antilles from the mouth of the Orinoco. At some point the two groups met in the northern Lesser Antilles or eastern Greater Antilles. The chapter explores what we know or can guess about this encounter and discusses the archaeological evidence for what emerged from it.

Following that, a chapter on the Saladoid phenomena discusses the movement of sedentary horticultural people from South America in the past 500 years B.C. The term *Saladoid* and other names for archaeological manifestations will be discussed in detail later, but at the most basic level it refers to a characteristic kind of pottery and associated archaeological remains that predominated in the Lesser Antilles and Puerto Rico until around A.D. 600. This time period has been the focus of some of the most concentrated archaeological research in the Lesser Antilles and Puerto Rico since the early 1970s (although compared to other areas in the Americas, the Caribbean has received relatively little archaeological attention), and the picture of this prehistoric period has changed substantially and become much more complex and interesting. One topic I deal with at some length is how and why there might be a contemporary use of two different assemblages of pottery, one the distinctive white-on-red painted pottery identified with the Saladoid migration and subsequent occupation and the other the zone-incised-crosshatched pottery associated with the site of La Hueca on the island of Vieques.

Chapter 4 explores the cultural interaction of the descendants of the Saladoid people with long-resident hunter-gatherer people who had lived in Hispaniola and Cuba for millennia. It also discusses the colonization of Jamaica and the Bahamas and deals with the emergence of Taíno complex societies.

Chapter 5 discusses the situation as it was shortly before the arrival of Europeans, commenting on the political geography of the various parts of the archipelago, the variability of societies from place to place, and the trends that seem to have been in motion before the arrival of the Europeans. In many parts of the islands, especially in the Greater Antilles and northern Lesser Antilles, the historical situation was certainly not static at the time of Columbus's arrival. In some areas things seem to have been changing rapidly even as the Europeans arrived.

The events of the early period of European contact are reviewed in Chapter 6, with attention paid to the differing histories of conquest in different places, in particular between the Greater and Lesser Antilles. By exploring events and reactions after the Europeans' arrival we attempt to understand deeper historical patterns of Caribbean life. Some of the main themes of the volume are revisited in the final chapter.

CHAPTER 2

THE FIRST HUMAN COLONIZATION OF THE CARIBBEAN

CARIBBEAN ENVIRONMENTS BEFORE HUMAN COLONIZATION

At the time of the first human visits, the Caribbean islands were vastly different places from what they are today and also very different from the environments that were there in 1492. This can be seen in the animals present on and around the islands, where many of the changes were brought about through human-caused extinctions and the transportation of new species to the islands. There were large flightless owls (*Ornimegalonyx oteroi* and others) in the Greater Antilles, bigger than any owls living today, and pygmy owls as well. There were also many genera of sloths (e.g., *Acratocnus, Megalocnus,* and *Parocnus*) and a range of other mammals, including seals, bats, large insectivores, herbivores, and rodents (Cunningham 1997; Woods 1989). Some of the large ground sloths may have grown to over 250 kg (MacPhee, White, and Woods 2000).

In general, islands have a less diverse range of species than the mainland because of the difficulties animals often faced in getting to the islands. This is a typical characteristic of island faunas — a limited diversity of species and a tendency for some species to take over niches or adapt in ways that produce odd results, for example, with the large flightless Moa birds of New Zealand, weighing up to 240 kg, or the late Pleistocene pygmy elephants of Indonesia (MacArthur and Wilson 1967).

The arrival of humans was bad news for the isolated faunas of the Caribbean islands. About 90% of the mammalian species that existed in the archipelago 20,000 years ago are now extinct. Some of the extinctions were probably caused by the post-Pleistocene climate change, but the first wave of human colonization around 6,000 years ago was much more significant. The arrival of Europeans caused another period of mass extinctions after 1492 (Cunningham 1997; Woods and Sergile 2001). For the people who first paddled their canoes out to the islands, however, the Caribbean ecosystems were rich and inviting. There were no terrestrial predators to threaten them and several species of large, slow prey. There were untouched coastal resources – fisheries, estuaries, and mangrove swamps.

The Caribbean environment differed from that of today in other respects. Sea levels had been much lower during the Pleistocene ice age, which ended around 12,000 years ago (Digerfeldt and Hendry 1987). It is difficult to be precise with sea levels in the Caribbean because of the islands tectonic dynamism; the histories of many Caribbean islands include accounts of drowned and raised settlements, as well as of earthquakes and volcanoes (Donovan and Jackson 1994). Reconstructing ancient shorelines is therefore very difficult. In general, however, at the end of the Pleistocene, a low ebb was around 120 m below today's mean sea level; the water had risen rapidly until around 6,000 years ago, when it was approximately 9–20 m lower. Thereafter the sea encroached upon the shore more slowly (Blanchon and Shaw 1995). For the people moving into the islands, the gradual flooding of the shoreline may have had an impact on their actions. On one hand, the rising sea level concentrated terrestrial fauna into a smaller space. At the time of the glacial maximum 18,000 years ago, Cuba, Yucatan, and Florida were all more than 50% larger than they are now and were nearing their present configuration at the time of the first colonization (Blanchon and Shaw 1995). On the other hand, rising levels would not have allowed mature reefs to develop offshore. It is possible, however, that the most significant impact of the rising sea level was on the mainland from which the first migrants came. Contracting land areas there would have forced the human population into smaller spaces and may have convinced some to venture out to unknown islands.

ORIGINS OF THE FIRST MIGRANTS

Apart from sites on Trinidad that will be discussed shortly, the earliest archaeological sites in the Caribbean date to around 4000 B.C. and are located in Cuba, Haiti, and the Dominican Republic. Table 2.1 gives radiocarbon determinations and calibrations for many of the early Caribbean dates, and Figure 2.1 shows the location of these sites.

The pattern of migration suggested by these early sites and dates is not one of gradual movement, of occupying one region and, eventually, as the need for space dictated, moving into adjacent areas. Rather, like most prehistoric migrations, the evidence suggests that people took long and rapid leaps of exploration. As a result, there is not a trail of gradual advance that would point backward to the point of origin of the migrants. In the Caribbean the earliest sites occupy an area 1,500 km wide with the earliest date – which has a calibrated range of 4350–4510 B.C. at Vignier III in Haiti – found more or less in the middle of that area (Figure 2.1).

In the absence of chronological clues as to the direction of migration, the search for the origins of the first Caribbean migrants has rested on stylistic and technological comparisons of stone artifacts from Caribbean sites with contemporary mainland assemblages. These comparisons offer evidence that Central America was the most likely source of the first migrants. An early example of this was William Coe's (1957) observation that large knives made on chert macroblades were found in both Central America and Haiti. Figure 2.2 compares an artifact from Belize illustrated by Coe (1957) to artifacts from Rouse's (1941b) excavations at Couri, Haiti.

Other researchers have examined alternative areas of origin for the first migrants to the Caribbean. Polish archaeologist Janusz K. Kosłowski, who, with his Cuban colleagues, carried out important research on preceramic periods in Cuba, discussed several possibilities in his *Preceramic Cultures in the Caribbean* (1974). Most significantly, Kosłowski carried out additional research at the site of Levisa I, in the Oriente province of Cuba. The site had been investigated earlier by Ernesto Tabío and his colleagues at the Academia de Ciencias de Cuba. The site of Levisa I is a rock shelter on the Río

TABLE 2.1. *Radiocarbon dates from early sites in the Greater Antilles and contemporary sites on the Yucatan peninsula*

Location	Lab No.	Site	Radiocarbon age				Calibrated date	
			Date B.P.	+/-	Calendar	A.D./B.C.	Cal range from (B.C.)*	Cal range to (B.C.)*
Cuba	Gd-252	Levisa	5140	170	-3190	B.C.	4250	3700
Cuba	**	Levisa	5050		-3100	B.C.	3980	3710
Cuba	SI-429	Residuario Fuenche	4000	150	-2050	B.C.	2900	2300
Cuba	Gd-204	Levisa	3460	160	-1510	B.C.	2030	1530
Cuba	Y-1764	Damajayabo	3250	100	-1300	B.C.	1670	1430
Cuba	SI-428	Resid.Fuenche	3110	200	-1160	B.C.	1650	1100
Cuba	SI-427	Resid.Fuenche	2510	200	-560	B.C.	850	390
Cuba	SI-426	Resid.Fuenche	2070	150	-120	B.C.	360	70 A.D.
Dominican Rep.	Y-1422	Mordan	4560	80	-2610	B.C.	3490	3100
Dominican Rep.	IVIC-5	Mordan	4400	170	-2450	B.C.	3340	2900
Dominican Rep.	Tx-54	Mordan	4140	130	-2190	B.C.	2900	2580
Dominican Rep.	I-6790	El Porvenir	2980	95	-1030	B.C.	1390	1090
Dominican Rep.	I-6615	El Porvenir	2855	90	-905	B.C.	1200	910
Haiti	Beta-**	Vignier III	5580	80	-3630	B.C.	4510	4350
Haiti	Beta-**	Vignier II	5270	100	-3320	B.C.	4240	3990
Haiti	Beta-**	Matelas	4370	90	-2420	B.C.	3300	2900
Haiti	Beta-**	Des Cahots	4340	80	-2390	B.C.	3100	2900

Provenance	Lab no.	Site	Date B.P.	±	Cal		1 sigma range	
Haiti	Beta-**	Phaeton	3260	70	−1310	B.C.	1630	1450
Haiti	Beta-**	Caberet	2280	80	−330	B.C.	410	200
Zone C	TX8295	Colha, Belize	2620	38	−670	B.C.	826	795
Zone C-1	CAMS8397	Colha	2780	60	−830	B.C.	1000	840
Zone C	CAMS8399	Colha	2930	60	−980	B.C.	1260	1050
Zone B4/top C	TX8106	Colha	2936	169	−986	B.C.	1390	930
Zone C	CAMS8398	Colha	2940	80	−990	B.C.	1300	1030
Zone C/B interface	TX7371	Colha	2950	100	−1000	B.C.	1320	1030
Base of Cobweb Clay Fill	Beta46785	Colha/Cobweb Swamp	2952	60	−1002	B.C.	1270	1060
Zone C	TX7459	Colha	3118	140	−1168	B.C.	1600	1160
Zone D	TX7460	Colha	3970	400	−2020	B.C.	3100	1900
Zone D	TX8020	Colha	4532	117	−2582	B.C.	3380	3030
Base of lower field	Beta64376	Colha/Cobweb Swamp	4630	60	−2680	B.C.	3510	3200
Cobweb Clay above basal marl	Beta39443	Cobweb Swamp 4BB	4723	65	−2773	B.C.	3220	3010

* Calibrations, (1 sigma range) ref. Stuiver and R. S. Kra (eds) Radiocarbon 28(2B):805-1030 (OxCal v.2.18).

** sample # not reported.

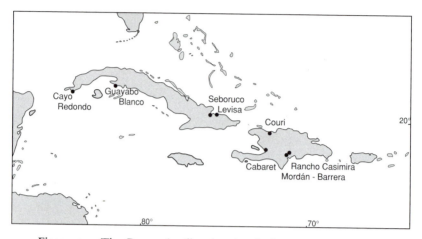

Figure 2.1. The Greater Antilles, showing the locations of the earliest sites.

Levisa, close to its mouth on the northeastern coast of Cuba (Figure 2.1). The shelter is about 7 m above the present level of the river and contains several meters of stratified deposits. Kosłowski identified eight cultural strata in the lower 1 m of the site. The two

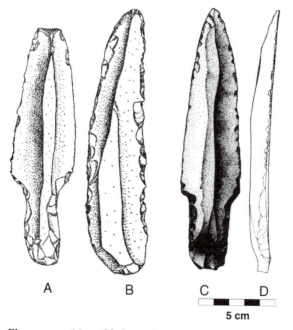

5 cm

Figure 2.2. Macroblade artifacts from Haiti and the Yucatan peninsula.

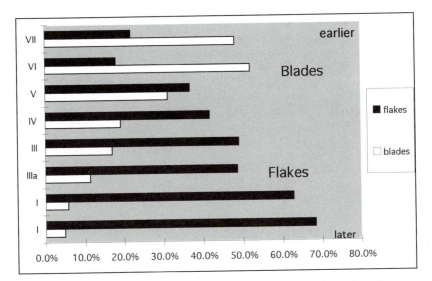

Figure 2.3. Graph showing the percentage of blades and flake tools at the site of Levisa I, from the oldest, Level VII, to the most recent, Level I (based on Kosłowski 1974:40–9).

radiocarbon dates from the lower part of the site have a calibrated range of 4250 to 3700 B.C. One of the most interesting aspects of change in this stratified deposit is the shift from stone tools made on blades to one made on chert flakes. Figure 2.3 shows the percentage of tools made on blades and flakes, with a steady increase in flake tools from the older to the younger levels and a corresponding decrease in blade tools (based on Kosłowski 1974:40–9). Another interesting change through time is that the use of conch shells (*Strombus gigas*) as a raw materials for tools became more prevalent in the younger strata.

Kosłowski examined similarities and differences between the Caribbean assemblages and those of Venezuela, Colombia, Panama, Costa Rica, Nicaragua, Honduras, Mexico, the Gulf Coast of the United States, and Florida. On the basis of this review, he found no strong technological parallels between the largely blade-based assemblages of Cuba and the roughly contemporaneous material from the surrounding mainlands. Although the comparative assemblages and chronological information available for the Yucatan peninsula were not well developed at the time of his writing, he did find the evidence from there suggestive: "The few and incomplete data that we have about the fluted points from the Central American region under study permit only the hypothetical assumption of the presence of the well-developed blade technique in this group of Palaeo-Indians" (Kozłowski 1974:24).

Since the time of Kozłowski's publication more has been learned of the lithic assemblages of the Yucatan. Richard MacNeish and his colleagues carried out the Belize Archaic Archaeological Reconnaissance (BAAR) in the 1970s and early 1980s. Many new archaic sites were found, in addition to those already known. Six sites were excavated by the BAAR (MacNeish and Nelken-Terner 1983; Zeitlin and Zeitlin 1996). The preservation of organic material at the sites they found was poor, however, so it was not possible to establish a precise chronology for the six archaeological phases they defined. The phase that showed the greatest similarities with the Greater Antillean assemblages was called Sand Hill, after the site of that name near the Belize River. The problem for Caribbean archaeologists, intrigued by the similarities in the large macroblade tools, was that the Sand Hill Phase was estimated date to about 6000–7500 B.C. – nearly 2,000 years earlier than the earliest Caribbean dates (Wilson, Iceland, and Hester 1998).

Additional archaeological research in the 1980s and 1990s has made it possible to refine this chronology. Preceramic strata from the site of Colha in Belize have been dated to before 3000 B.C., with paleobotanical evidence for clearance before that (Hester, Shafer, and Eaton 1994; Jones 1994). The Colha deposits contained lithic production areas, with many macroblade tools, as well as smaller blades, prepared blade cores, and other evidence for their manufacture. Similar large macroblades, sometimes pointed and some with usewear, have been found in central Belize at sites such as Sand Hill and Ladyville (Hester *et al.* 1994). A characteristic "dagger" form, with unmodified converging distal tip and bifacially trimmed base similar to those in Figure 2.2, is known in both the Greater Antilles (Veloz Maggiolo 1976:281) and Belize, but it should be noted that none of the Belize specimens have been found in well-dated contexts.

There have been suggestions for some time that the Yucatan was the most likely place of origin for the first people who moved into the Greater Antilles; the recent discoveries in Belize strengthen the case. It is also important to consider the rarity of lithic assemblages containing macroblade tools, or even blade manufacturing technology at all, for the time period and areas in question. Finally, the lack of evidence for human occupation in the Lesser Antilles island chain at this time makes a point of origin near the western end of the archipelago most probable.

It should be noted that Richard Callaghan has carried out extensive studies of the winds and currents of the Caribbean, examining the likelihood of reaching the islands from various points on the mainland (Callaghan 1985, 1995). He found that drift voyages from South America had the highest probability of success for reaching the Greater Antilles. Further research (Callaghan 1992) suggested that direct canoe travel between the Greater Antilles and South America was possible, and was probably faster and safer than travel all the way through the Lesser Antillean island chain. This has bearing for understanding the early colonization of the islands, and is also important for understanding the external contacts that continued through the entire prehistory of the region.

THE EARLIEST SETTLEMENTS

Since the early 1900s archaeologists had found sites with large blade tools and without pottery, but there was little evidence to tell definitively whether the sites were early or late. In 1912, Jacques Roumain reported on the site of Cabaret near Port-au-Prince in Haiti. Roumain attributed the lithics from the site to the "Ciboney," a hunter-gatherer group said by some early Spanish chroniclers to have been present in western Cuba at the time of the conquest. Thus it was not clear whether the remains Roumain found were to be attributed to the earliest, or some, of the latest indigenous people of the region. The Danish archaeologist Gudmund Hatt also described comparable lithic assemblages from the Dominican Republic (Hatt 1924), and Cuban archaeologist A. Nuñez Jimenez (1948) described the artifacts from the site of Seboruco, in eastern Cuba.

Rouse has used the broad heading "Lithic age" to categorize archaeological assemblages of flaked stone tools without ground

stone or pottery (Rouse 1992:51) and has designated these earliest blade-tool assemblages Casimiran Casimiroid, after the site of
Casimira in the Dominican Republic that he and José Cruxent
excavated (Cruxent and Rouse 1969). Kozłowski (1974) used the
term *Seboruco-Mordán Culture* to refer to the earliest archaeological
manifestations, and Veloz Maggiolo (1972:74) and others have used
the term *Paleoindio*. Most recently, Cuban archaeologists have categorized such sites as being representative of the earliest hunter or
"cazadores" economic phase (Febles *et al.* 1995).

Despite the relatively large number of sites known from this
period, the lives of these earliest inhabitants are not well understood (Newsom and Wing 2004:29–34; Ortega and Guerrero 1985;
Pantel 1988). Several of the best known sites – such as the Seboruco
locality in eastern Cuba and both Casimira and Barrera-Mordán
in the Dominican Republic – are primarily lithic workshops, and
although they provide good evidence for stone tool manufacture,
they reveal little about other aspects of life.

The Levisa I locality in the Oriente province of Cuba (Figure 2.1)
was very likely a habitation site and contains a wide range of archaeological materials. The site is in a rock shelter near the mouth of
the Río Levisa (although its distance from the coast would likely
have been greater during this period of occupation) and it contains
at least eight stratified levels of cultural deposits. From these deposits
and other sites Cuban archaeologists have reconstructed aspects of
the diet of the first migrants (Febles *et al.* 1995). The most remarkable characteristic of this diet, compared to that of later Caribbean
people, is its reliance on large animals such as seals, manatee, and sea
turtles. The land mammals, such as the hutia, were hunted and the
largest land animals, such as the large sloths, were probably hunted
to extinction. Fishing was apparently not practiced and evidence for
the collection of shellfish, although present, does not indicate that
it played a substantial role in the diet (Febles *et al.* 1995; Kozłowski
1974).

Through time, there was a gradual shift away from large land
and sea animals. With many generations of experience in the
Greater Antillean environments, people began to look to the rich
coastal environments for a larger fraction of their animal protein. By

around 2000 B.C. evidence for fishing and especially shellfish collection becomes much more conspicuous in the archaeological record (Newsom and Wing 2004). The descendants of the first immigrants may have been forced into this change by declines in the populations of larger prey species. As noted, some of the easiest prey, such as the large sloths, became extinct. It is also likely that as they settled into the new environment and through dozens of successive generations gained deeper knowledge of the ecological communities of which they were now a part, their skill in gathering food increased and their diet became more diverse.

In the stone tools at Levisa we can see another change characteristic of the early centuries of adaptation to the Greater Antilles. Through time people made fewer and fewer blades and used flakes as the basis for most of their stone implements. In the earliest levels at Levisa I, about 50% of the lithics analyzed were blades (see Figure 2.4). In the youngest levels of the shelter, about 5% were blades and the majority were flakes (Kozłowski 1974:table V). This change in stone tool technology was not the result of lack of good raw material. Cuba and Hispaniola had chert sources that were equal in quality to those of Central America (Pantel 1988; Veloz Maggiolo 1972).

The change from blade to flake technology has been viewed by Kozłowski as evidence of technological "degeneration." Similar observations of technological simplification have been made in other prehistoric cases, often in island settings. For example, in Polynesia the first people to colonize many of the islands used pottery of a style called Lapita, but through time made less and less of the pottery until the manufacture of ceramics was completely abandoned (Kirch 1997). A similar case for "technological degeneration" is argued for the pottery-making people of the Caribbean who arrived in the Lesser Antilles nearly two millennia after this change in lithic technology took place. As will be discussed in Chapter 3, the earliest pottery used by Caribbean people was finer and harder and made with greater technological sophistication than the ceramics of subsequent periods (Rouse 1992).

Rather than view the changes in lithic technology that took place in the first 2,000 years of human occupation of the Greater Antilles as degeneration, we must consider the remarkable accommodations to new settings the first migrants were making in this period. They had moved from a mainland that had been occupied for nearly 10,000 years, containing a variety of large mammals and predators, to an area with few large land mammals and no large terrestrial predators apart from themselves. Some tropical plants were similar, but many were different, requiring generations of exploring, learning, teaching, and building the detailed knowledge that characterizes most tropical peoples' relationship with their environments. This process of adaptation presented new problems and called for a different toolkit. Through the nearly six millennia of human occupation of the islands, stone tools became less and less important, whereas objects made of shell, wood, basketry, ground stone, clay, and cotton took on new functions and new importance.

For between 1,000 and 2,000 years, the first colonizers had the Greater Antilles to themselves. They moved across Cuba to Hispaniola to Puerto Rico and beyond, establishing small sites of less than 1 ha in area (Veloz Maggiolo 1972). During that long time – a span of perhaps 75 to 100 generations of descendants – the groups in the different islands and areas became culturally distinct, one from the other. Some suggestions of this are to be seen in the stone tools, as has been noted by several scholars (Kozlowski 1974; Pantel 1988; Rouse 1992; Rouse and Cruxent 1963). It is as yet unclear whether these differences are regional, chronological, or both or what they may mean in terms of other aspects of life – other technologies, economy, settlement pattern, language, and so forth. Careful excavations and detailed comparisons of sites from this period are still needed to help understand the detailed character of the adjustments made in new environments, the nature and extent of cultural divergence through time, and the impact of continued interaction with the Central American mainland, if it existed.

NEW MIGRATIONS AROUND 2000 B.C.

The earliest inhabitants of the Greater Antilles, for all their variability and distinctive ways of dealing with different environments, were probably very similar in their history, way of life, languages,

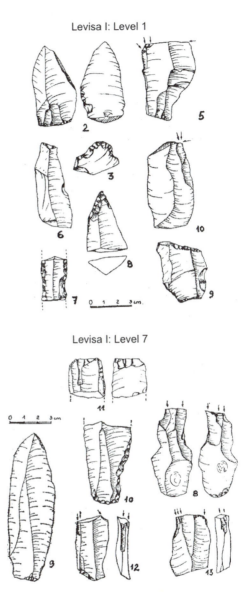

Figure 2.4. Artifacts from the site of Levisa I, Levels I and VII (after Kosłowski 1974:figures 8 and 11).

and other elements of their culture. That measure of cultural homogeneity would end forever in the Caribbean sometime before 2000 B.C., when new groups moved into the region. Forever afterward the archipelago would be home to people with different cultures and points of origins, and the islands would be the sites of their interaction and mutual accommodation.

The encounters of culturally different groups are thus one of the most important recurring phenomena in Caribbean prehistory and history. Sometimes these encounters were brief and overwhelmingly one sided, as with the European conquest of the Greater Antilles. More often they were very protracted and resulted in extensive change to all the groups involved in the encounter. As will be seen in later periods, cultural contact and interaction was many times a powerful force for change. It helps to account for technological change, for example, in the dissemination and probable invention of pottery in several places. Culture contact and interaction also helps us understand the cultural geography of the region, with some frontiers maintained for centuries. Finally, this theme of diverse cultures in contact helps us to understand the social and political changes that resulted in complex societies in the Caribbean. But at this early point in the colonization of the Caribbean, the story is of two groups of hunter-gatherers, ultimately of Central and South American origins, meeting in the northern Lesser Antilles and eastern Greater Antilles.

The initial movement of people from South America to islands adjacent to the mainland started several thousand years before the colonization of the Lesser Antilles began in earnest. The earliest evidence for human activity is an isolated find of a bifacially flaked spear point that is comparable to the early Holocene Joboid lithics from the mainland (Rouse and Cruxent 1963). In the late Pleistocene both Trinidad and Tobago were part of the mainland; afterward the glacial maximum sea levels rose, creating the Gulf of Paria along Trinidad's west coast. At the time of the spear point's use, Trinidad may still have been connected to the mainland by an isthmus between what is now the southern coast and northern Venezuela. The last connection of the island to the mainland was breached sometime in the early Holocene (Boomert 2000:39–46). Today the island of Trinidad is just a few kilometers from the mainland, and its flora and fauna – and to some extent its history of human habitation – reflect that. Today Trinidad is culturally and historically part of the West Indies, but from the time it was first inhabited by people until the time of European conquest, it had the closest ties to the mainland of all the Caribbean islands. As such it served as a first, short-step Lesser Antillean archipelago. This was the apparently the case for the first permanent migration of people into the islands.

BANWARI TRACE, TRINIDAD

Around 6000 B.C. people from the South American mainland began to live on Trinidad. As with the earliest sites in the Greater Antilles, people established their settlements in environments that were similar to those they had exploited on the mainland. The site of Banwari Trace is on a hill above the swampy channels of the Oropuche and Coora Rivers in southwestern Trinidad. It is nearly 10 km from the coast, and when the site was first occupied it would have been even farther from the sea (Boomert 2000; Boomert and Harris 1988; Harris 1973). Today the marine estuaries and mangrove swamps extend about 2 km inland from the Gulf of Paria, creating a complex and rich series of littoral, esturine, and freshwater environments.

Like most sites from this early migration into the Lesser Antilles, Banwari Trace is a shell midden. It is about 30 m in diameter and contains over 2 m of deposits at its deepest point (Boomert 2000; Boomert and Harris 1988; Harris 1973). Its earliest strata show that people collected shellfish from several environmental zones, including the nearby freshwater rivers and swamps, estuaries, and sea coast. They also caught a variety of crabs from freshwater and esturine swamps and mangroves (Harris 1973, 1976).

As with a great many sites in the Caribbean, Banwari Trace was investigated because of the efforts of local people, interested in their islands' history and prehistory. Peter Harris and the members of the Trinidad and Tobago Historical Society (South Section) excavated the site of Banwari Trace on weekends in 1969 and 1970. Harris presented the results at the Fourth International Congress for the Study of Pre-Columbian Cultures of the Lesser Antilles, held in St. Lucia in the summer of 1971, and published an article on the finds in the proceedings of that congress (Harris 1973). These congresses or meetings have been held every two years since the first one was held in Fort-de-France, Martinique, in 1961. They are held in a different place each time, so that participants will have a chance to see different islands and visit important archaeological sites. Since the early 1960s some changes have taken place in the meetings. They have become larger and more difficult to put on, and the *Proceedings* volumes – incorporating all of the papers presented – are much thicker. But these meetings still have the strong and active participation of local amateur archaeologists, who make up a large percentage of the group that has developed into the International Association of Caribbean Archaeologists.

Between Banwari Trace and the Gulf of Paria is the site of St. John. It was occupied at the same time as Banwari Trace and has very similar archaeological remains. In both sites little use is made of deep sea resources, and in both there is a general shift from the use of terrestrial animals toward the use of foods from marine environments, particularly inshore and esturine species (Boomert 2000:58). In reporting some of the food remains from Banwari Trace, Peter Harris has characterized this economic shift as one from hunting/fishing/collecting to one of fishing/hunting/collecting (Harris 1973). The distinction may seem subtle, but what it suggests is a change, over 2,000 years, in a whole range cultural patterns that allowed people who had for millennia lived along the river systems of South America to live in environments where marine resources were abundant and important (Newsom and Wing 2004:75–113). Their seasonal calendar of rains and available resources would have to have changed, and the focus of their economy shifted to the rocky coasts, shallow and deep reefs, and open waters. Through time, even into late prehistoric times in the Lesser Antilles, marine foods continue to play a larger and larger role in the diet (Wing 1989).

The fact that people were able to collect the foods and raw materials they did from so many parts of this complex set of marine environments argues strongly that they used canoes. Their assemblages of stone artifacts included the tools of canoe makers, and all of the inhabitants of the mainland who were most closely related to them lived along the rivers of the northern South America, probably including the Orinoco and the river systems of the Guyanas to the southeast. Like most lowland South American people, these related groups used canoes as well.

The artifacts from Banwari Trace and St. John include tools of bone and stone related to fishing and collecting, canoe building, plant processing, and general cutting and scraping. The ground stone artifacts used by people at Banwari and related sites are distinctive, and they remained in use for a long time in the Lesser Antilles. Many of the ground stone tools appear to have been used for pounding and processing hard or fibrous vegetable material. These include large (30 cm) pestles as well as smaller ones, mortars or anvils, manos, and grooved axes. They also made a characteristic sort of ground stone tool that is modified through grinding or pounding only on its edges (Boomert 2000; Harris 1972, 1973, 1976). Harris (1973:122) describes them as "[o]riginally water-rounded flat stones, all share in common evidence of coarse grinding round the edge...." These were the most commonly found ground stone tools on Banwari Trace, St. John's, and the related site of Poonah Road, followed by pestles and hammerstones. Figure 2.5 illustrates two of these "edge grinder" artifacts (nos. 1 and 2), as well as a grooved axe (3) and utilized flakes (4) (after Boomert 2000:figure 8).

The flaked stone artifacts from these sites, and most of preceramic sites in the Lesser Antilles, are less distinctive than the ground stone. Most are small flakes or fragments of chert, made by striking small nodules or fragments of chert between a hammerstone and an anvil. This technique is termed *bipolar reduction* and tends to produce flakes that are small and irregular, but still useful, as sharp edges for a variety of cutting and scraping uses. Flakes often show some degree of crushing on one or both ends. Small angular fragments or "shatter" without usable sharp edges are produced by this bipolar technique (Walker 1990:69–72). The chert tools from Banwari Trace have these characteristics, and according to Harris (1973:119) the raw material was obtained from nearby sources.

Bone tools were also preserved at Banwari Trace and St. John's in large numbers (Harris 1973:119). The most common were sharpened bone tips for hunting or fishing spears. They range in size from about 2 to 15 cm in length. Another type of artifact was made of bone or tooth, sharpened symmetrically at both ends. Boomert has identified these as double-pointed fishhooks, similar to those used by the Warao people, the historic and present-day inhabitants of the

Orinoco River delta (2000:58). Archaeologists also found several needles and needle fragments.

The archaeological remains at sites like Banwari Trace and St. John's are a tiny fraction of the material goods that surrounded the people who lived there. Even with this small and fragmentary record, and despite the seven millennia separating us from them, we can understand something of their lives through comparisons to lowland South American groups known through ethnography or historical records. With these analogies in mind, the fragments of stone and bone tools – especially things like ground stone axes and needles – are best seen as tools used in the creation of what the Banwari people would have seen as their material goods, things such as canoes, houses, hammocks, baskets, spears, burden baskets, nets, digging tools, jewelry, clothing, toys, and musical instruments. The great majority of these things are made of wood, fiber, feathers, leather, and other things that almost never survive long in an archaeological site (Braun and Roe 1995; Steward 1948).

On neighboring Tobago, 32 km away from the northeast corner of Trinidad and easily visible from the Trinidad's Northern Range, there are archaeological sites similar to these early sites on Trinidad. Arie Boomert conducted excavations at the site of Milford 1 in the mid-1980s and found faunal remains reflecting a focus on the sea, shallow reefs, mangroves, and ground and flaked stone artifacts comparable to the Banwarian sites on Trinidad (Boomert 2000: 75–7).

Under the classification system long used and refined by Irving Rouse (see Rouse 1992:31–3, 50), these sites fall within the Ortoiroid series. The name was taken from the site of Ortoire on Trinidad, which is actually a more recent site than Banwari Trace and the other sites just discussed. Ortoire dates to about cal 700–1000 B.C. The name Ortoiroid has been fairly widely used in the Lesser Antilles to describe comparable preceramic assemblages, however, and its use is retained here. Boomert (2000:54–5) categorized nearly all the preceramic sites on Trinidad and Tobago within the subseries Banwarian Ortoiroid, signifying that despite their individual differences, the sites are comparable to Banwari Trace. Specifically, they are sites of less than 1 ha that share the stone tool kit

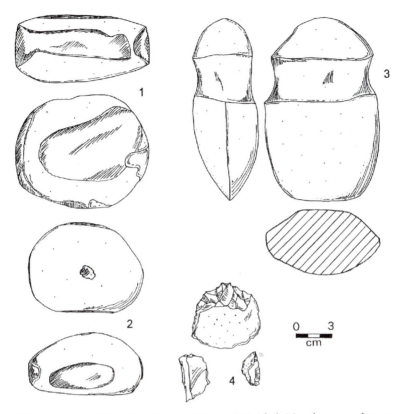

Figure 2.5. Artifacts from Banwari Trace, Trinidad. Numbers 1 and 2 are side or edge grinders, 3 is a grooved axe, and 4 are utilized flakes. After Boomert (2000:figure 9).

of Banwari Trace and reflect a focus on economic resources of the coasts, mangroves, and shallow reefs.

ORIGINS OF THE PEOPLE WHO COLONIZED
THE LESSER ANTILLES

From where did the people who lived at Banwari Trace and related sites come? In looking for similar environmental settings, in which people with a comparable technology could base an economy on similar kinds of foods, the most likely sources include the Venezuelan coast to the west of the mouth of the Orinoco, the Orinoco

Delta itself, and the coast to the east of the Orinoco, extending to the southeast. Of those, the ones with the strongest chronological and archaeological correspondences are with a series of shell middens in northwest Guyana known as the Alaka complex (Boomert 2000:68–74; Evans and Meggers 1960; Versteeg 1998; Williams 1985). This cluster of sites is between 200 and 400 km to the southeast of Trinidad, with the many islands and channels of the Orinoco Delta in between. The sites are located on rises at the edges of coastal swamps and marshes where the inland tropical forests meet extensive mangrove swamps and estuaries that extend many kilometers to the sea. As with Banwari Trace and St. Johns, these sites were first occupied at a time when sea levels were still rising. The encroaching sea changed the distribution of saline, brackish, and freshwater environments within the coastal swamps, and these changes are sometimes reflected in the faunal stratigraphies of the sites.

Boomert divides the Alaka complex into two chronological units (2000:69–72). Early Alaka spans from cal 6000 B.C. to cal 4000 B.C., and Late Alaka continues until about 1500 BC. As can be seen on Figure 2.6, the Alaka complex dates (shown on the right side of the illustration and labeled "Guyanas") coincide closely with those from Trinidad and Tobago (just to the left of the Guyanas on Figure 2.6). Alaka complex technology is also similar to that of the Trinidad sites, with ground stone implements and an informal lithic industry characterized by bipolar processing of stone raw material. The distinctive side or edge grinders of Banwari Trace and similar sites do not appear at the Alaka sites, although related tool types – hammerstones, ground stone choppers, mortars, and pestles – are present (Boomert 2000:71–2; Evans and Meggers 1960:25–54). Although the artifacts from the two groups of sites are not entirely interchangeable, the correspondences are is still close enough to see the Alaka complex as the relative of Banwari and the probable source of the population.

Another group of sites that is related to the Banwarian sites on Trinidad, although somewhat later in date, is the El Conchero complex of the Paria peninsula and the Venezuelan coast east of the Gulf of Paria (Boomert 2000:72–4; Cruxent and Rouse 1982; Sanoja 1980). Both the food remains and stone tools are similar to the

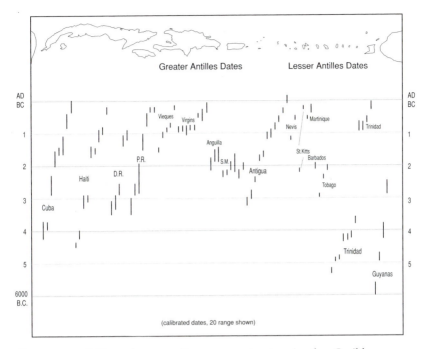

Figure 2.6. Calibrated ranges for preceramic sites in the Caribbean, arranged roughly in spatial order with Cuba on the left and Trinidad on the right. The preceramic dates for each island are sorted with the earliest dates on the left.

Banwarian and Alaka complex sites. The sites are shell middens with informal flaked stone artifacts made from a variety of high- and low-quality raw material. The ground stone inventory is very comparable to those at Banwari and Alaka as well, with side grinders, mortars, pestles, hammerstones, and probably grooved axes (Boomert 2000:73).

COLONIZING THE LESSER ANTILLES

The sea voyage from the mainland to Trinidad is just 13 km and Tobago is another 32 km beyond Trinidad. Tobago is always in sight for a person making the crossing by canoe. The next step along the archipelago, however, from Trinidad or Tobago to Grenada, is more difficult. It is 125 km distant and out of sight beneath the horizon,

even from high in the hills on a clear day. It is difficult to understand
why people took their boats out beyond the horizon, but they have,
nevertheless, done it countless times in human history. However, it
is not always necessary to see an island or land mass to know it is
there. The flights of birds out to sea often signal land beyond the
horizon, and many of the Caribbean islands create their own plume
of clouds, trailing to the leeward side. Also, very rarely, atmospheric
conditions make it possible to see far beyond the horizon, when a
temperature inversion acts as an atmospheric mirror, reflecting an
image of very distant islands. It is a widely known phenomenon,
especially among seamen, and was even noted by Aristotle. Thomas
Jefferson commented on it in his *Notes on the State of Virginia* in 1782
(1801:80–1):

> Having had occasion to mention the particular situation of
> Monticello for other purposes, I will just take notice that its ele-
> vation affords an opportunity of seeing a phænomenon which is
> rare at land, though frequent at sea. The seamen call it looming.
> Philosophy is as yet in the rear of the seamen, for so far from
> having accounted for it, she has not given it a name. Its principal
> effect is to make distant objects appear larger, in opposition to
> the general law of vision, by which they are diminished.

So with Grenada almost within sight, it was probably not a complete leap of faith for the first explorers to go away from the mainland. Sometime after about 3000 B.C. they paddled their canoes
north from Trinidad and Tobago and moved up the island chain,
for having made that first difficult step off of South America's con-
tinental shelf, each island thereafter was in sight of the previous one
all the way to Cuba.

The movement into the Lesser Antilles was not a gradual process,
with people colonizing one island and staying there until economic
or social problems made it easier to move to the next one than to stay.
Rather, they went long distances, exploring and leaving evidence of
their presence in archaeological remains. This pattern is typical of
most human migrations; when people first came into the Americas
they did not colonize the place slowly; instead, they went as far

as one physically can very quickly. One of the earliest sites in the Americas, Monte Verde, is in southern Chile, at the southern end of South America, and 16,000 km from their presumed points of entry at the Bering land bridge or northeastern coasts.

The evidence for the exploration of the Lesser Antilles is not extensive, and only a few of the sites that were eventually occupied have been examined in detail. However, even taking into account the superimposition of sites by later occupations or destruction through human or natural action, it does not appear that the preceramic occupation of the Lesser Antilles was large in terms of numbers of sites or numbers of people. Most of the sites are small shell scatters with some flaked and ground stone tools. These camps seem to be places where canoe-mobile people visited, lived for a while, perhaps on a seasonal basis, and fished and collected coastal resources. Looking at a few of these sites, both early and late in the sequence of occupation, brings at least part of this colonization effort into focus.

The site cluster at Krum Bay, on the island of St. Thomas in the Virgin Islands, has been relatively well studied and is representative of many of the preceramic sites in the Lesser Antilles and Puerto Rico (Lundberg 1989; see also Bullen and Sleight 1963; Lundberg 1980, 1991). It is located just south of the St. Thomas airport in a little bay that looks out onto the half-kilometer-wide channel between St. Thomas and Water Island. Krum Bay is one of several small bays tucked amid the hills and crags of the igneous deposits that make up the south coast of St. Thomas. The little bay itself is narrow and sheltered. There were three small concentrations of shells and other archaeological remains when the Danish archaeologist Gudmund Hatt visited the site in 1923. He described the shell heaps as having a noticeable quantity of red ochre, long stone axes, and hammerstones and speculated that the remains "represented the remnants of a culture, earlier and more primitive" than other sites he had seen (Hatt 1924:31). By the time Ripley Bullen and Frederick Sleight carried out excavations in 1960, roads had cut across the site, leaving an intact section of about 10 × 25 m. The original extent of the main shell scatter, not recorded by earlier authors, would not have been much larger, perhaps 35 m in diameter at most.

The artifacts from Krum Bay, and many related preceramic sites, are easy enough to overlook that archaeologist Theodoor de Booy, who visited the site in 1917, noted that there was "not even the smallest Indian specimen to indicate that the shell-heap had been made by the aborigines of the island" (Bullen and Sleight 1963:7). Most of the flaked and ground stone tools were made of the local basalts and other igneous rocks, close in color and texture to the surrounding unmodified stone. There were clearly many artifacts there, however, made to consistent designs to perform particular tasks. They are similar in function to the Banwari Trace tools, including flaked tools for cutting and edge or side grinders, hammerstones, mortars. and pestles for crushing and pounding. They also made and used stone axes and a type of roughly flaked celt-shaped biface about 15 to 25 cm in length (Lundberg 1989:96–139). A finely worked pendant fragment and some polished stone beads were found in the oldest strata of the site. The beads were about 4 mm in diameter and were made of several different kinds of raw material, probably imported to St. Thomas (Lundberg 1989:104–5). The working of ground, pecked, and polished stone reached a very high level in the Lesser Antilles in the period before ceramics came into use. Figures 2.7, 2.8, and 2.9 show ground stone artifacts from the Lesser Antilles.

Krum Bay dates from about cal 100–1000 B.C., and so is a relatively late site in the sequence of preceramic sites in the Lesser Antilles. One of the earliest sites between Trinidad and Puerto Rico is Sugar Factory Pier, on St. Kitts. The excavations at Sugar Factory Pier were not extensive, but they did produce a radiocarbon date of cal 2090–2210 B.C. and an array of artifacts similar to those found both on Trinidad and Krum Bay, including edge grinders, conch shell tools, basalt pestles, and simple flaked tools made of chert brought over from the island of Antigua, about 85 km away (Armstrong 1978; Goodwin 1978b).

Another well-excavated preceramic site is Norman Estate, on St. Martin (Hofman and Hoogland 1999). Radiocarbon dates from the site range from cal 2362 to cal 1742 B.C., so it has many characteristics comparable with other Ortoiroid sites but also shows some variability. It is located on a low saddle in the northern part of the French part of St. Martin, about 1.5 km from the sea both to the east

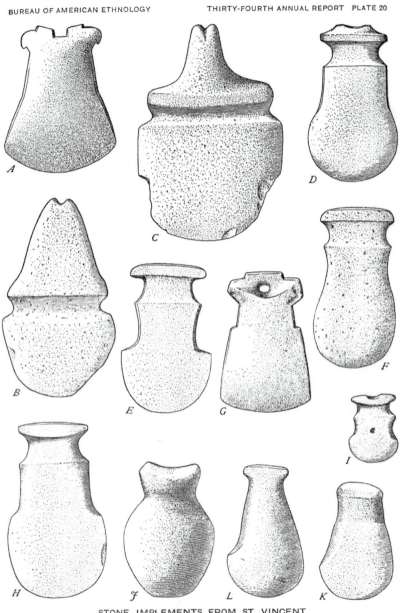

STONE IMPLEMENTS FROM ST. VINCENT
B, 7.75 inches; *C*, 8.44 inches; *E*, 6 inches; *J*, 5.25 inches; *L*, 5.5 inches.

Figure 2.7. Ground stone axes from St. Vincent (from Fewkes 1922).

Figure 2.8. Artifacts C and D are eccentric stone objects from Guadeloupe (Fewkes 1922:plate 81) in the Guesde Collection, Berlin Museum. Artifact A is a Casimiran shell pendant from Haiti (after Rouse 1992:figure 17). Artifact B is a stone ring or bowl from Guadeloupe (Fewkes 1922:plate 75).

and west (Knippenberg 1999a). The most conspicuous part of the site is a shell midden originally about 30 m in length, which is now cut by a road and ditch. The main part of the archaeological deposit is about 50 cm in thickness and is partially buried by overburden from the road. The site contains artifacts of chert, with a less formal set of ground, pecked, or battered stone tools that have been found at other sites of comparable age. The ground or worn stone tools show edge wear from hammering or grinding. The majority of the chert at Norman Estate comes from the Long Island site on Antigua (Knippenberg 1999b). The occupants of the site collected shellfish,

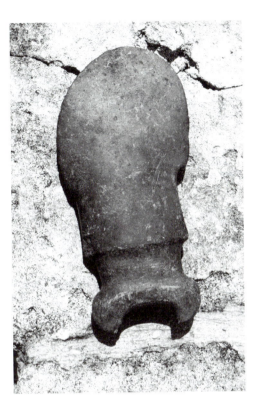

Figure 2.9. Ground stone axe from the Museum of Antigua and Barbuda, 28 cm in length.

including *Arca zebra*, from the reefs on the western side of the island and *Codakia orbicularis* and other sand/mud species from mud flats to either the east or west of the site. They apparently did not eat *Cittarium pica* or crabs (Brokke 1999). They were quite capable of catching fish from the deep and shallow reefs, relying mostly on the parrotfish (Scaridae)' and grunts (Haemulidae) (Nokkert 1999). The habits of the fish they caught and their numbers at Norman Estate suggest that the preceramic inhabitants used fish traps, much as people do today in the West Indies (Nokkert 1999:58; Wing and Reitz 1982).

As the wide distribution of chert from Antigua throughout the Lesser Antilles indicates, the island seems to have been a center for early occupation and resource exploitation. It has many more known preceramic sites than all of the other Lesser Antilles together, with 43 (Davis 2000:81). There are several sites older than 2000 B.C.

The earliest is the Little Deep Site, dating to 3106 B.C. (Nicholson 1994:12). Another important early site is Twenty Hill, dating to 2910 B.C. (Nicholson 1994:12, 1976). Nearly all of the archaeological research on Antigua, for the preceramic as for later periods, has been encouraged, abetted, or carried out by Desmond Nicholson, the long-time director of the Museum of Antigua and Barbuda. Nicholson also helped to organize the first Congresses of the International Association for Caribbean Archaeology and has often served on its board of directors.

What is most interesting about these early sites on Antigua is that the lithic technology employed at them is not the expedient bipolar reduction seen at the Ortoiroid sites discussed thus far. Rather, the people living there were striking blades off of prepared cores. This blade technology is much more closely related to that brought into the Greater Antilles by the first migrants from Central America.

Dave Davis noted the similarity between the early Antiguan lithics and those of the Greater Antilles when analyzing the blades (Figure 2.10) recovered from the Jolly Beach site in Antigua (Davis 1974, 1993, 2000). He concluded, "It is my feeling at the present time that the Barrera I complex, or a culture derived from it in the Greater Antilles, is the forebear of the earliest occupation of Antigua" (Davis 1974:69–70). At the Jolly Beach site itself he saw artifacts that he felt were comparable to the Ortoiroid sites. Others have questioned the comparison with, arguing that the high-quality chert on Antigua made it more likely that people working the stone would produce some blades simply by chance. Arie Boomert sees more connections with the Alaka complex than with the macroblade complexes of the Greater Antilles: "the Jolly Beach technique of percussion flaking is quite similar to that of the Ortoiroid series and any seemingly more sophisticated flint artifacts would appear to result from the excellent quality of the raw material available in Antigua rather than from a more refined tradition of flint knapping" (Boomert 2000:79).

Boomert and Davis may both be correct. The site of Jolly Beach, with a radiocarbon date of cal 1865–1685 B.C., may reflect the interaction and fusion of both technological traditions. Jolly Beach has both blades and ground stone artifacts but far fewer ground stone implements than would typically be found on an Ortoiroid site. It

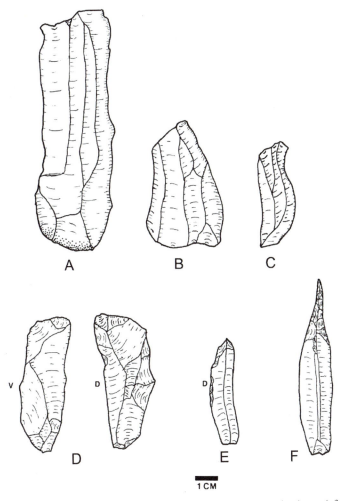

Figure 2.10. Lithics from the Jolly Beach site on Antigua (after Davis 2000:Figures 9 and 10). Artifacts A, B, and C are classified by Davis as blade cores, and D, E, and F are retouched blades from Jolly Beach.

also exhibits some characteristics that are atypical for the Ortoiroid sites. For example, the people living at Jolly Beach did not eat the West Indian Top Shell (*Cittarium pica*), a source of food found at most other sites. For example, at the site of Caño Hondo on the island of Vieques, with radiocarbon dates from cal 1130–685 B.C., *Cittarium pica* accounts for 72% of the shell weights of molluscs (Figuerado

1976:251). They also did not eat land crabs (Davis 2000:90–1). It is not clear that land crabs were ever a preferred food in the preceramic, however.

If the early sites on Antigua and elsewhere in the northern Lesser Antilles represent the eastward extension of the people who first moved from Yucatan to Cuba, where are their sites on Puerto Rico and the Virgin Islands? Several interesting possibilities have emerged in recent years. Some have early radiocarbon dates but few associated artifacts, as at Paso del Indio in north-central Puerto Rico. There, in deep backhoe trenches dug in research on a much later site, investigators found hearths over 5 m below the surface with charcoal dated to cal 3500–3200 B.C. (García Goyco, Maurás, Crespo, and Walker *et al.* 1995). Those dates fit well with an emerging picture of the area between Puerto Rico and Antigua as a zone of interaction for people coming from the western Greater Antilles and those from Trinidad and South America via the Lesser Antilles.

With that sort of interaction scenario in mind, one of the most exciting new sites is that of Maruca, in southern Puerto Rico (Rodríguez 1999). It is located on a terrace of the Río Matilde, about 1.5 km from the sea near the town of Ponce. The site was first excavated by Jesús S. Figueroa Lugo and later by prominent Puerto Rican archaeologists Juan J. Ortiz Aguilú, Agamemnon G. Pantel Tekakis, and Miguel A. Rodríguez López. A strong group of specialists, including Edwin Crespo, Diane Hansen, Jorge Febles, Jeff Walker, Juan Gonzalez, Antonio Curet, and Lee Newsom worked on materials from the site. The early occupations at Maruca date in the third millennium B.C., from cal 2890 to 1945 B.C. There are also later dates showing a continuing occupation until cal 395 B.C.

What makes Maruca so remarkable is that its artifacts can clearly be related to the large and early assemblages of the Dominican Republic, Haiti, and Cuba, with large blades, blade cores, scrapers, and flake tools. It also has connections to the east, and Dr. Jeff Walker has suggested that some of the chert may in fact come from Antigua's largest chert quarry on Long Island. Dr. Jorge Febles, a Cuban archaeologist and lithic specialist who has carried out a great deal of research on these early assemblages throughout the

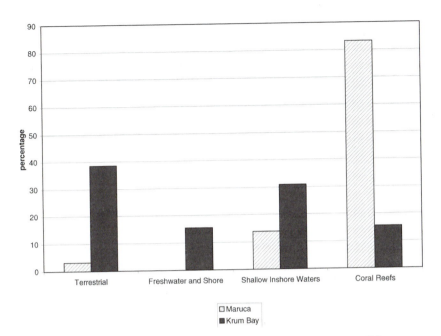

Figure 2.11. Comparison of faunal remains from Maruca, Puerto Rico, and Krum Bay, Virgin Islands, by habitat.

Caribbean, identified these correspondences with the other early sites in the Dominican Republic, Haiti, and Cuba. He also suggests that there could be connections with lithic traditions from the west coast of Florida and the lower Mississippi Valley (Rodríguez 1999:27). There were also many ground stone tools at Maruca, with many reminiscent of the Banwari Trace assemblage, with mortars, conical pestles, and stones with battering and wear on the edges. They also made tools of conch shell (*Strombus gigas*) in a style comparable to artifacts from Cuba, including large projectile points, hand picks, and carved and drilled shell ornaments (Rodríguez 1999: 28–9).

Also, as can be seen in Figure 2.11, the patterns of faunal exploitation at Maruca are very different from those at Krum Bay. At Maruca people focused their attention on the coral reefs, where at Krum Bay they used a wider variety of habitats (Newsom and Wing 2004: table 7.2a).

SUMMARY

Figure 2.6 shows the calibrated ranges for preceramic sites in the Caribbean, arranged roughly in spatial order with Cuba on the left and Trinidad on the right. The preceramic dates for each island are sorted with the earliest dates on the left.

The dates from the Greater Antilles, on the left, show that people entered the islands about cal 4000 B.C. The earliest dates are in Cuba and Haiti, and slightly later dating sites are shown in the Dominican Republic and Puerto Rico. These early occupations were certainly more substantial than the archaeological evidence indicates at present. Many sites from this period have probably been submerged by sea-level rise and isostatic movement of the islands. Others have been destroyed by subsequent natural processes or human activity. Others have yet to be found and investigated. With more sites, and careful excavation, the archaeological understanding of the lives of these early inhabitants will improve, but the basic timing of their arrival will likely stay in about the range shown on Figure 2.6.

On the other end of the Caribbean archipelago, people moved into Trinidad around cal 5000 B.C. The dates from Banwari Trace and St. John, and scattered finds on Trinidad, suggest a larger occupation. There on Trinidad, however, people seem to have stayed for the next 2,000 years. The earliest dates from neighboring Tobago, from the site of Milford 1, are at around 3000 B.C. (Boomert 2000:75–7). It was the step to Tobago that launched the real exploration of the Lesser Antilles. Between 3000 and 2000 B.C., people moved through the Lesser Antilles. They moved north through the islands, selecting for their camps places with fringing shallow reefs. They also accomplished the difficult passage out to Barbados, 150 km out in the Atlantic Ocean, straight into the trade winds and equatorial currents – a voyage that is more of a feat than getting from Tobago to Grenada.

Some time in the period between 3000 and 2000 B.C., these two groups came into contact with each other in the northern Lesser Antilles or Puerto Rico. It was the first of many such encounters in the Caribbean, in which two groups of very different culture, language, and history met. In this earliest case it is difficult to describe the nature of the relationship between them. The fraction of their material culture that has survived is so small and the sorts of artifacts – mostly informal stone tools – do not provide a sensitive reflection of culture change. Nevertheless, there is some evidence that their interaction resulted in the exchange of ideas and technology, if not some degree of cultural integration. Sites such as Maruca and Jolly Beach show archaeological ties to both Trinidad and the Greater Antilles and may be models for the kind of sites we should be looking for. Other sites, such as Whitehead's Bluff and other sites on Anguilla with suggestions of lithic blade technology (Crock, Petersen, and Douglas 1995), may be displaying similar signatures of interaction.

Encounters between peoples of different cultures are a recurring theme in the history of the Caribbean. In this first instance of culture contact, despite their similarity in technology and economy, the cultural and linguistic gulf between the two groups would have been immense. This raises the possibility is that there was some interaction between these groups, but that in general they maintained some distance between themselves. Between Anguilla and Puerto Rico are the Virgin Islands, Vieques, and Culebra. The earliest dates on those islands are about cal 1500 B.C., many centuries after the first encounters of these groups would have taken place. That lack of evidence for earlier dates is not convincing, however, given the relatively little archaeological research that has been carried out on these early sites.

At a general level, the encounter between people of Central American and South America descent led to a fundamental change in the preceramic Caribbean. As Marcio Veloz Maggiolo concluded (1976:304):

> From the point of view of chronological divisions of the preagricultural pottery makers (preagroalfareras) in the Antilles, there is evidence for two great periods: the Early Archaic or Paleoarchaic, which was a period of adapting mainland technologies to the island environments; and the Archaic, a period of settling in, local evolution, and the development of mechanisms of appropriation that were specific to the Caribbean. During this period the population of the groups increased and they began the important process of techno-economic hybridization. . . .

After this encounter had begun, there were no major movements of people into the Caribbean for between 1,000 and 2,000 years. There was probably continued contact with the mainland, but during this period the most evident historical process was the development of distinct regional adaptations. Archaeologists have debated the extent and boundaries of identifiable "complexes," based on the archaeological characteristics of sites or groups of sites scattered from Cuba to Antigua. For the Greater Antillean series termed Casimiroid, Rouse (1992:49–70) defined three subseries – the Casimiran, Courian, and Redondan. The first, Casimiran, refers to the first people to occupy both Cuba and Hispaniola, and the Redondan and Courian subseries refer to the later periods on each island, respectively. The date of the transition between subseries is around 2000 B.C.

Veloz Maggiolo (1976:242–5) defines five subtraditions, also named for regions or type sites – Banwaroide, Cordilleroide, Mordanoide, Guayaboide, and, finally, the subtradition into which they all eventually resolved (albeit with regional variants), the Hibridoide.

Recalling Bill Keegan's advice to "avoid the 'OID,'" it may be best to follow that advice here. The danger is that the work of drawing boundaries in space or time (an essential heuristic task in archaeology) blinds us to the more important changes going on in the past. There are in fact two processes at work. On one hand, there was the process of technological and economic hybridization observed by Veloz Maggiolo that continued until almost all of the people in the archipelago were using a similar, efficient, way of living in the complex Caribbean environment. On the other hand, they were developing identifiable regional characteristics and undoubtedly undergoing linguistic and cultural change through the generations as well. In Caribbean history the processes of economic and technological synthesis – and cultural differentiation – are always in tension. Far from being a "melting pot," the historical forces in the Caribbean have generally stimulated cultural differentiation, as much in the preceramic as at present (Wilson 1993).

CHAPTER 3

THE SALADOID PHENOMENON

Based on the archaeological evidence in the Lesser Antilles and Puerto Rico, the migration of a new group of people into the Caribbean in the last few centuries B.C. was very obvious. In contrast to the chipped and ground stone assemblages of the preceramic people, the elaborate ceramics of the new arrivals, with their brilliant white-and-red designs, were impossible to miss. Also in contrast with earlier occupations, the new colonists lived in large, permanent villages, grew crops, and interacted with their environments in different ways. Rouse classified their distinctive pottery as belonging to the Saladoid series, named after the site of Saladero in Venezuela (Boomert 2000:217–51; Keegan 2000; Rouse 1992:30–7).

Because of the contrast of this new archaeological evidence with the earlier sites, the arrival of Saladoid people was viewed as a major migration of South American people up the Lesser Antillean chain, overwhelming, displacing, or absorbing the previous occupants. Saladoid sites with remarkably similar archaeological characteristics have been found on most of the islands. Caribbean archaeologists have viewed this as a wave of migration creating a Saladoid horizon, which swept through the Antilles as far as eastern Dominican Republic and had a major impact on all subsequent Caribbean history.

In recent years this picture has become somewhat more complicated. It now seems likely that the migrating group was more diverse than previously thought, possibly involving multiple groups.

The process of migration probably involved voyages of reconnaissance, short-lived settlements, and retreats. Moreover, the interactions with Archaic people who were already living in the islands probably played a much more important role than was thought in shaping the Saladoid advance, their adaptation to the Caribbean environment, and Saladoid culture itself (Chanlatte 2003; Keegan n.d.; Rodríguez Ramos 2005).

This chapter explores the long trajectory of population movement, from its complex beginnings in South America to the point at which colonization stalled for centuries along the eastern shores of the Dominican Republic. Both the points of origin and the processes of movement – the complexities of which are only now being recognized – are considered. One of the most striking examples of this complexity is the enigmatic presence of archaeological remains called La Hueca, or Huecoid, on Puerto Rico, Vieques, and a few other places. As will be discussed, La Hueca shows that groups in the early Saladoid period were not as homogeneous as they once seemed, and it invites us to consider the significance of artifactual differences in terms of their cultural meanings and importance.

The migration of Saladoid people into the Caribbean is one of the most fascinating events in Caribbean prehistory and it has received a great deal of attention by archaeologists (Siegel 1989; Wilson 1997). A good understanding of this period is crucial for shedding light on the main themes emphasized in this volume – cultural diversity and its significance in Caribbean prehistory, the emergence of complex societies, the development of multi-island interaction spheres in the Lesser Antilles, and the importance of extra-Caribbean contacts.

MAINLAND ORIGINS

Where did the Saladoid people come from? This has been a source of heated debate in Caribbean archaeology since the 1950s. Some, including Donald Lathrap and Irving Rouse, saw the ancestors of the Saladoid people coming from the Amazon basin, crossing into the Orinoco drainage, and eventually moving into the Caribbean

(Lathrap 1970; Rouse 1991). Others, including Betty Meggers, Clifford Evans, Mario Sanoja, and Iraida Vargas, saw their origins to the west, in the large Colombian River valleys at the feet of the Andes (Meggers and Evans 1961, 1978; Sanoja 1983). These differences in interpretation are understandable, and they illustrate the difficulties of approaching a very complex set of archaeological questions with a still very fragmentary and partial archaeological record. The variables include multiple possible points of origin, the possibility of systematic problems with the contamination of radiocarbon dates from the Middle Orinoco, and perennial difficulty in archaeology of comparing stylistic and technological modes of poorly dated ceramic assemblages from far-flung locations and trying to decide which is related to which. Long geographic extrapolations are necessary because in many large areas in lowland South America there is a dearth of archaological research.

Nevertheless, with the benefit of ongoing research, the origins of the indigenous people of the Caribbean are clearer than they were in the past (Boomert 2000; Oliver 1998; Vargas 1990). In light of this, we can reexamine the evidence for the mainland origins of the Saladoid people.

From a long career in lowland South America, particularly in the upper reaches of the Amazon basin, Lathrap (1970) constructed a scenario in which the Saladoid and Barrancoid originated in the Amazon. He argued that they crossed into the Orinoco drainage at the Casiquiare Canal, an area of marsh and small river channels that connects the upper reaches of the Río Negro and the Upper Orinoco (Figure 3.1). Across this canal, Lathrap and others reasoned, people could paddle or pull their canoes from one river system to the other.

Boomert (2000:115 and section 2.1) sees other possibilities for crossing this divide, arguing that ethnohistoric evidence supports use of the Pirara Portage between the Río Branco and the Rupununi/Essequibo systems in southern Guyana (Figure 3.1). As will be discussed, the archaeological evidence for Saladoid people using this latter route is also stronger than it is for the Casiquiare Canal passage. There are other close connections between northern tributaries of the Amazon and the rivers flowing north from the Guiana High-lands, and it is possible that several routes of movement across the divide were used.

Lathrap saw the strong connections between the first Saladoid people in the Orinoco and the pottery makers from high in the Amazon basin in eastern Peru. His reconstruction was that

> [t]he distribution of these complexes around the whole periph-ery of the Upper Amazon Basin suggests that this homeland is to be sought in the Central Amazon near the confluence of the Upper Amazon, the Negro and the Madeira. The ceramic evidence points to a pattern of population movement simi-lar to that indicated by the distribution of the more diver-gent branches of Arawakan. It is of greatest interest that the Antillean Saladoid ceramics can be attributed without reason-able doubt to the speakers of Proto-Taino, the northernmost of the non-Maipuran Arawakan families, while there is every reason to believe that the Nazaretequi tradition was the work of the speakers of Proto-Amuesha. (Lathrap 1970:112)

Betty Meggers and Clifford Evans (1978) and Sanoja and Vargas (1978, 1983) saw Saladoid and Barrancoid origins in the north-western part of South America, in particular in the major river systems draining the Andean highlands of Columbia, Ecuador, and Peru. Meggers, who with Evans worked in many parts of lowland South America, from the mouth of the Amazon to the shadows of the Andes in Ecuador, proposed an extensive "Amazonian Zoned Hachure" tradition that includes ceramic complexes from Puerto Hormiga in northern Colombia to the mouth of the Amazon. In this tradition she includes both La Gruta, the earliest Saladoid pot-tery in the Orinoco, and Tutishcainyo ceramics from the Upper Amazon (Meggers 1987, 1991).

One thing is clear: the Saladoid ceramic series, and what we have come to understand as Saladoid culture, did not develop *in situ* in the Orinoco. The people making these ceramics certainly changed and developed them once they were there, but Saladoid-related ceramics came in the Orinoco drainage as well-developed and highly sophisticated ceramic complexes (Boomert 2000; Oliver 1989; Roosevelt 1997). Although the Alaka people of Guyana and

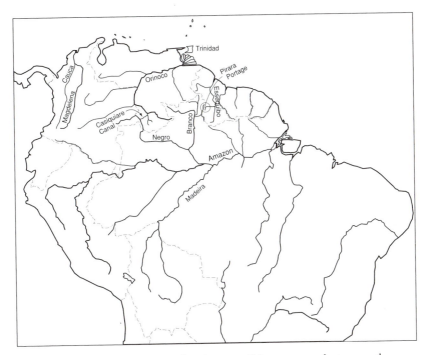

Figure 3.1. South America, showing possible passages between the Amazon and Orinoco drainages.

the Lower Orinoco, did make pottery in their later period, it was comparatively crude and unrelated to the Saladoid ceramics either stylistically or technologically.

The picture that has been emerging since the early 1980s is that the Orinoco basin was a zone of intensive cultural contact and inter-action for thousands of years, and particularly so in the last 2,500 years B.C. Given the substantial influences coming in from outside the region, from both the river systems and Llanos to the west and the Amazon basin to the south, it now seems much less productive to debate whether the origins of the first ceramics-using people of the Caribbean were strictly from one region or another. The Middle and Lower Orinoco formed the crucible in which Saladoid, Barran-coid, and many other archaeological cultures developed, and there was usually a high degree of interaction, even over large distances, among the many groups living there.

What this means is that the archaeological situation in the Orinoco drainage and the northeastern South America is very complex, much more complex than what happened later in the Caribbean. The multiple overlapping and intermixed pottery traditions clearly reflect a cultural geography with multiple interacting groups. An example of this is the widespread and long-lived distribution of the sort of Cedeñoid pottery excavated by Alberta Zucchi and Kay Tarble at the sites of Agüerito and Cedeño in the Middle Orinoco (Zucchi and Tarble 1984; Zucchi, Tarble, and Vaz 1984). These two sites are near one another about 600 km by river from the sites of Saladero and Barrancas and another 600 km from the divide between the Orinoco and Amazon drainages. Cedeñoid pottery is present in the Middle Orinoco at about the same time as Saladoid pottery, and in fact Cedeñoid occurs in small quantities in many of the sites that are predominantly Saladoid. Also, both Cedeñoid and Saladoid pottery occur as minority or "trade" pottery at important Middle Orinoco sites such as Corozal, Ronquín, and La Gruta (Boomert 2000:109–10; Roosevelt 1997:155–62; Zucchi 1991). As Roosevelt notes, "Thus, early Corozal seems a period of rapid, extensive, and parallel change in several aspects of ancient lifeways. ... The great distance between the new Corozal pottery wares, shapes, and decorations and the older Saladoid-Barrancoid pottery on the one hand, and the evidence for interaction between pottery of the different traditions on the other, suggest that people of different geographic origins may have come together in the same community ..." (Roosevelt 1997:161).

This suggests that the period from 1000 B.C. until the first centuries A.D. was a time of flux and change in the Orinoco, involving several groups who were trading long distances and sometimes living together in the same places (Heckenberger 2002; Zucchi 2002). Roosevelt suggests an analogy to modern times in the lowlands, in which individuals or groups might migrate long distances in search of better economic possibilities (1997:161). Many others have documented the complex cultural landscape of the lowlands, with patterns of occupation, trade, and population movement that would be extremely difficult to reconstruct on the basis of archaeological data (Basso 1995; DeBoer 1981; Forte 1996; Whitehead 1988; Wilbert 1996).

Another way of trying to unravel the complexities of the cultural interactions of the Orinoco in the last 2,500 years B.C. is to use the techniques of historical linguistics. For our purposes the most important of these techniques is linguistic glottochronology, which attempts estimate the point in time at which two modern languages diverged from a common ancestor. In northern South America, given the cultural complexity, movement of groups, and difficulties in interpreting the archaeological record, it is very difficult to employ these methods with any precision, and for that reason we do not rely heavily on it here. Oliver (1989) has done the most careful and thorough job with this in reconstructing the Arawakan expansion into northwestern Venezuela and eastern Colombia. He divides the expansion of Arawakan speakers into northern South America into three major stages (pp. 173–82). In the first stage, one group of proto-Maipuran speakers (the presumed ancestors of the people who went into the Caribbean) diverged from proto-Arawakan in the central Amazon before 1500 to 2600 B.C. and moved into the Upper Orinoco and Upper Río Branco. From there one group of them continued westward into the Llanos of western Venezuela and Lake Maracaibo, whereas another remained in the Upper and Middle Orinoco. In Oliver's second stage, the group that had remained in the Orinoco moved to the Orinoco Delta, some moving out into the Antilles, and others moving southeastward into the coastal Guyanas. In his stage three, further movement and linguistic differentiation takes place in western Venezuela and the lower Amazon, but by that time the groups that became the historically known people of the Caribbean – the Taíno and Island Caribs – had diverged from their mainland relatives.

In considering the mainland origins of the Saladoid people, it is also important to recognize the important relationship between the Saladoid people and another group who lived in the Lower Orinoco at the same time and who are generally known by their Barrancoid pottery style. The relationship between the Barrancoid and Saladoid groups in the Lesser Antilles has important implications for the prehistory of the Antilles, because interactions with Barrancoid people occurred from A.D. 200 to 600 and continued afterward. It influenced the initial movement of people into Antilles and had an ongoing influence through interaction with the mainland for centuries afterward (Heckenberger 2002). Barrancoid influence can be seen in Caribbean pottery after A.D. 600, even in the Greater Antilles, as potters moved away from painting flat surfaces to suing clay more sculpturally, with heavy modeling and deep, broadline incision.

Although the Saladoid ceramic tradition had deeper roots in the Orinoco basin, extending back to about 2500 B.C., the period of Barrancoid interaction was a powerful historical force motivating change. This interaction led to one of the fruitful periods of creativity and cultural expression that I believe are a part of a pattern – that periods of cultural interaction are also periods of great creativity and innovation in the Caribbean (and probably in human societies generally). As Arie Boomert notes, "Undeniably, Barrancoid ceramics form the artistic climax of pre-Columbian culture in the Caribbean, being both highly aesthetic and imaginative" (2000:118). Sanoja and Vargas (1978:97) describe Barrancoid art of the period as containing a wealth of decorative motifs, "representing mythical beings that were part human and part animal (bats, felines, fish, etc.), which indicate a rich ceremonial life and the existence of an animist religion in which the deities or natural spirits had a great importance."

Around 800 B.C. people making Barrancoid pottery show up in the Lower Orinoco, in the region around the present-day city of Barrancas, where the Orinoco begins to break up into the dozens of rivers of the 200-km-wide Orinoco Delta. Their occupation seems to be intrusive rather than a local development, and their origins have been the subject of considerable debate (Lathrap 1970; Rouse and Cruxent 1963; Sanoja and Vargas 1983). Boomert's recent review (2000:93–125) considers the problems of poor dates and uneven archaeological information and concludes that the Central Llanos of Venezuela and Colombia are the most likely immediate source, but that the northern Andes and the river systems of northern Colombia are still possible sources of influence. Thus in the period of cultural interaction in the Middle and Lower Orinoco in the last millennium B.C. both Andean and Amazonian ancestries may have had some expression and influence on the cultures of the Caribbean (Heckenberger 2002; Rouse 1991). The Barrancoid influence extended into the southern Lesser Antilles until A.D. 600–800 and extended as far as the Leeward Islands.

SALADOID EXPLORATIONS INTO THE CARIBBEAN

As noted at the beginning of this chapter, Saladoid archaeological sites are distinctive because of their white-on-red painted ceramics (Figure 3.2). In the following discussion we encounter the question of how to interpret the differences between this kind of pottery and another kind found in early Saladoid sites, and this returns us to the question of classification. One sort of pottery has been mentioned briefly above. It is characterized by white-on-red (which is often abbreviated WOR) and polychrome painting and has modeled and incised ornamentation on the rims or handles called adornos (Figure 3.3 shows complete vessels from the site of Sorcé on Vieques, redrawn from Chanlatte [1979, 1981]). Incision or some sort of painting is found on nearly half of this pottery. The pottery vessels included bowls, dishes, and jars, and they also made pottery griddles and other specialized pieces, for example, potstands and incense burners. The other kind of pottery has been called Huecoid or Huecan Saladoid and tends to be thinner and unpainted. Some vessel forms are unique to the Huecoid assemblages and unknown from Saladoid sites.

A source of some a great deal of difficulty in understanding the relationship of Saladoid and Huecoid is that one kind of decoration on ceramics, often found on early Saladoid sites, is similar to, and perhaps related to, Huecoid ceramics. That decorative mode is called zone-incised-crosshatched (abbreviated ZIC) and refers to zones on the vessel surface that are delineated with marked incision and filled with a fine crosshatching of lighter incision. ZIC decoration is used at the site of La Hueca but on vessel forms that are not usually found in Saladoid sites. Also, the zone-incised decoration at La Hueca is also not as refined and well executed as in the early Saladoid sites. It was done when the clay was wetter and more malleable and the patterning was not as regular. The problem, as we shall see in some detail in this chapter, lies in understanding the cultural and historical

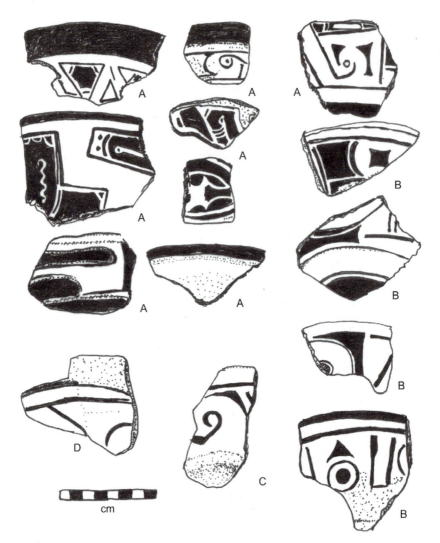

Figure 3.2. White-on-red pottery from several Saladoid sites: A, Hichmans, Nevis; B, Hacienda Grande, Puerto Rico (after Rouse and Alegría 1990); C, Trants, Montserrat (after Peterson and Watters 1991); D, Tutu Village, St. Thomas (after Righter and Lundberg 1991).

significance of the Huecoid assemblages, the Saladoid assemblages characterized by WOR pottery, and the presence of Huecoid-like ZIC pottery in the early Saladoid assemblages. In the following discussion we will use the term *Huecoid* to refer to the ceramics from

Figure 3.3. White-on-red painted ceramics from the site of Sorcé, Vieques (after Chanlatte 1976, 1979, 1981).

La Hueca, Punta Candelaro, and related sites. Huecan Saladoid will refer to the ZIC pottery typically found in Saladoid sites.

THE FIRST SALADOID EXPLORERS

Before radiocarbon dating began to be used in the Caribbean in the 1950s, there was no way to anchor a relative archaeological chronology to absolute calendar years. There were also few ways to determine whether a phenomenon like the regionwide appearance of Saladoid sites occurred as a sudden wave or a protracted trickle of people. As more radiocarbon dates have accumulated, even through the 1990s, it appears that it might have been a relatively coherent movement but one preceded by earlier explorations, perhaps by different groups of people.

Figure 3.4 shows the distribution of the Saladoid sites with the earliest radiocarbon dates in the Lesser Antilles and Puerto Rico (the figure shows those sites dated earlier than 100 B.C. based on the midpoints of each date's calibrated 2-σ range). These dates carry with them varying degrees of confidence and, as with all radiocarbon assays, are subject to many potential problems. New sites are being studied, and others, including some of those mentioned, are subject to ongoing research, so this is a very provisional set of data from which to draw some tentative impressions. Nevertheless, some possible patterns may be observed. First, there is no suggestion of a gradual migratory wave of settlement moving from south to north in the Lesser Antilles, with, for example, beachheads on Grenada, the Grenadines, St. Vincent, and St. Lucia. On the basis of current research and existing dates, the early Saladoid migrants bypassed the southernmost islands. Instead, the earliest dates are further north, on St. Martin, Montserrat, Martinique, and Puerto Rico. Second, these early dates do not appear to be just the earliest of a large number of dated sites and deposits. In other words, they do not seem to represent the arrival of the founders of lasting and expanding Saladoid occupations. Instead, they seem to predate the sites that came afterward by several centuries in some cases. This suggests that the earliest Saladoid strategy in the Caribbean was one of exploration and isolated, small-scale, and possibly intermittently occupied settlements.

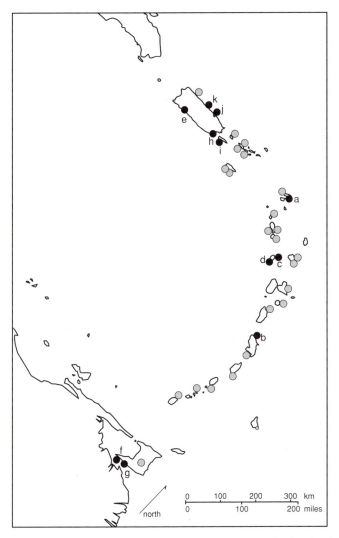

Figure 3.4. Distribution of early Saladoid sites. Early dated Saladoid sites are shown as black circles and labeled. Smaller gray circles show later Saladoid sites. For the early sites, the following labels apply: a, Hope Estate, St. Martin; b, Fond Brulé, Martinique; c, Trants, Montserrat; d, Radio Antilles, Montserrat; e, Tecla, Puerto Rico; f, Cedros, Trinidad; g, Palo Seco, Trinidad; h, Punta Candelero, Puerto Rico; i, Sorcé, Vieques; j, Convento, Puerto Rico; k, Maisabel, Puerto Rico.

A third potential pattern is one of variability in the earliest Saladoid sites. Although they have similarities, there are also significant differences to be seen among the 11 early sites shown in Figure 3.4. Three of the earliest are the Hope Estate site on St. Martin, Trants on the island of Montserrat, and Cedros on Trinidad's southwestern peninsula. Some further discussion of these sites may help illuminate some of the characteristics of this period.

The site of Hope Estate is in the hills of northern St. Martin, about 2 km from the sea both to the east and the west. It sits at about 100 m above sea level. It has been the subject of research by many archaeologists, including Bonnissent, Haviser, Henocq, Hofman, Hoogland, Richier, and Weydert, among others. The site was occupied several times in prehistory, but it is the first occupation that we are most concerned with here. Hoogland and Hofman carried out excavations at the site in 1993 and reconstructed three main phases of occupation. The earliest period occupation is thought to date from about cal 400–300 B.C. (Hoogland 1999:129–47).

The ceramics from this early component are Huecoid – unpainted pottery decorated with incision, including ZIC and some modeling (Bonnissent 1995; Hofman 1999). This pottery also contained a rare decorative mode called zone-incised punctate, in which instead of filling incised decorative areas with fine crosshatching, the potter filled them with punctations. The incised areas are bounded by curvilinear lines and filled with either crosshatching or punctation (see Figure 3.5). Simple, unrestricted bowls and jars are most common, and the assemblage also contains restricted contours. In Hofman's study (1999:159–65) the average vessel diameter is 25.3 cm, and the average wall thickness was 6.8 mm. Rims were simple, typically rounded, and sometimes flattened. Some vessels were ornamented with modeled adornos, usually zoomorphs with round eyes. A very small fraction of the pottery from this occupation phase, about 0.2%, have decoration associated with Cedrosan Saladoid ceramics – white-on-red painting and red slips – but these artifacts may be intrusive from higher in the site's complex stratigraphy (Hoogland 1999:143–7).

Hofman and Hoogland interpret the second stratigraphic unit of the site to be a predominantly Cedrosan Saladoid occupation. The decorative modes on the ceramics include white-on-red and

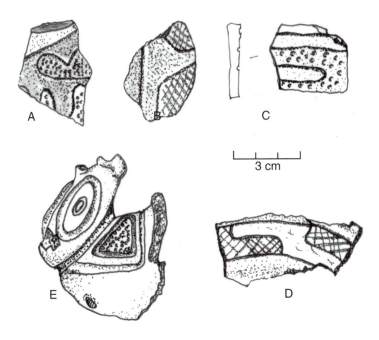

Figure 3.5. Early zone-incised crosshatched and zone-incised punctate sherds from Saladoid sites. A, B, and C are from Hope Estate (after Hofman and Hoogland 1991). Sherd D is from Trants on Montserrat (after Petersen and Watters 1991:305), and E is from Morel on Guadeloupe (after Durand and Petitjean Roget 1991).

polychrome painting (about 20% of the decorated sherds) and some zone-incised crosshatching (about 10% of the decorated sherds). Over 50% of decorated sherds are incised, and there is also some modeling. Within this stratigraphic unit seven zone-incised punctate sherds were found (of 12,928), but they were deemed to be a product of mixing during site formation processes. For the most part, the artifacts from this second component, which Hoogland estimated to date to about cal A.D. 450–600, were typical for a Saladoid site in the northern Lesser Antilles of similar age. As noted, it had both WOR and ZIC ceramics, griddles, highly variable chert artifacts, and beads and other artifacts of exotic stone (Haviser 1999). The site probably had a succession of houses dating from the earliest occupation onward (Hoogland 1999:figure 11.13).

In summary, Hope Estate is a site with a very early occupation that contains an unusual component that is exclusively Huecoid in character. It contains zone-incised punctate ceramics that are found in only a few other sites. After a long period of abandonment, Hope Estate is reoccupied with a more typical Saladoid settlement, containing both ZIC and WOR ceramics.

The site of Trants, on the east coast of Montserrat, is another very early Saladoid site but with some characteristics that separate it from Hope Estate. It does have pottery that are similar to Huecoid ceramic assemblages – i.e., they have unpainted vessels sometime with zone-incised crosshatched decoration – but unlike at Hope Estate, Trants does not have a discreet deposit of this pottery without white-on-red pottery present, nor did it have zone-incised punctate ceramics. Instead, the ZIC and WOR ceramics are consistently found together, and Petersen and Watters (1991:292) note,

> some of the WOR and ZIC vessels show common techniques and even nearly identical motifs between different site areas on the basis of surface and subsurface finds. For example, the earliest deposits at the site thus far identified, dated ca. 480–440 B.C. in fields 8 and 9, share a common unslipped, bowl form with a flanged rim that was decorated using a common form of broad line ZIC and a similar punctate adorno, along with WOR decorated vessels. The former occurrence, among others suggests that these areas were occupied more or less contemporaneously by people sharing very similar, if not precisely identical ceramic styles.

From their descriptions and profile drawings, it seems as if the largest part of the midden at Trants, stratum B, dates to the last century B.C. to about A.D. 200 (see also Petersen 1995; Watters 1994; Watters and Petersen 1995). However, the investigators believe that the site's basic configuration, a 200 × 300 m oval midden ringing a central plaza, was established before 400 B.C., and early dates come from several parts of the site (Petersen, Bartone, and Watters 1995:44).

The interesting thing to note here is the difference between the Huecoid ceramics of La Hueca and Hope Estate and the Huecan Saladoid ceramics from other Saladoid sites. Although superficially similar, they have different meanings. The Huecoid ceramics (and almost certainly the people who made them) are clearly distinct from the ZIC ceramics found among WOR ceramics in Saladoid sites. The latter are copied from, inspired by, or derived from the same source as the Huecoid pottery, but as Watters and Petersen note, the Huecan Saladoid ceramics are stylistically and technically very close to the contemporary WOR pottery with which they are found. Rather than reflecting some cultural difference, they seem to be a specialty ware within the more general Saladoid assemblage.

Of all the early Saladoid sites, the closest one to the South American mainland is the site of Cedros, on the southwestern peninsula of the island of Trinidad. It looks south onto the channel called the Serpent's Mouth and to the mainland 15 km away. Like many early Saladoid sites, it is located on a rise with a commanding view about 200 m back from the coast. It is close to freshwater swamps and mangrove areas and also close to the geothermal features called mud volcanoes that are common on the southwest coast. It is hard to know the site's original extent, but the relatively modest size of the remaining midden suggests that it was not large, perhaps consisting of a few houses, with the trash midden on the slopes of the hill down-wind from the houses (Boomert 2000:264). The early component probably dates to around 100 to 300 B.C. (Boomert 2000:127–45), so it probably postdates the sites just mentioned by a century or two.

Cedros is another classic example of the early Saladoid sites, and its name was given to Rouse's Cedrosan Saladoid subseries (1992:77–85). Boomert analyzed the pottery excavated at Cedros and the nearby site of Palo Seco and provides a detailed description (Boomert 2000:127–45; see also Harris 1978). Of the decorated sherds, 51% were painted in some fashion, and 14% had white-on-red painting. Others had simple red or orange paint, white or black paint alone, or polychrome painting. Sixteen percent of the decorated sherds had ZIC decoration and another 19% had other kinds of incising. Boomert identified seven common vessel forms and seven rare forms. The common forms are mostly unrestricted bowls with rim forms varying from thickening and flanges to elaborate compound rims. The functions performed by the vessels included storage, cooking, food preparation that did not include heating, serving, and transport of the vessels' contents (Boomert 2000:136–9).

As may be seen from these three sites, there is considerable diversity among the early Saladoid sites. Of critical importance is the relationship between the two dominant decorative styles of the pottery – white-on-red painting and zoned incision. What does the presence of these two modes mean in terms of the human processes of exploration, colonization, and population movement, and how should sites like La Hueca and those similar to it be seen in Caribbean prehistory?

LA HUECA AND THE EARLY SALADOID

In the late 1970s, Luís Chanlatte Baik and his colleagues at the University of Puerto Rico made one of the most dramatic and important archaeological discoveries of the late twentieth century at the site on La Hueca, on the island of Vieques, just off the coast of southeastern Puerto Rico (Chanlatte 1981; Chanlatte and Narganes 1980). Until that time the ZIC pottery (which is called Huecan Saladoid in this discussion) that was typically found in Saladoid archaeological sites was thought by nearly all Caribbean archaeologists to be a minority constituent of the Saladoid assemblages, diagnostic of the early Saladoid period. At the site of La Hueca, however, only ceramics affiliated with this ZIC tradition were found, without the white-on-red pottery characteristic of the abundant Saladoid sites of the Lesser Antilles and Puerto Rico (Chanlatte and Narganes 2005). Moreover, La Hueca produced spectacular examples of small carvings in exotic stone and shell – frogs, bats, amulets, beads, disks, and raptorial birds holding human heads (Figure 3.6).

Some sites, including Punta Candelero, La Hueca, and the earliest levels of Hope Estate, have only early Huecoid ceramics. There are other early sites that have comparable assemblages, including decorative modes with curvilinear incised zones filled with punctations, or zoned hachure. Similar ceramics have been found at Morel (Durand and Petitjean Roget 1991:53–8) and Anse Patat (Hofman 1999:311) and perhaps Folle Anse on Guadeloupe and El Convento and Maisabel on Puerto Rico (Siegel 1992). For some of these sites it is likely that the early Huecoid material occurred alone, without white-on-red pottery or other Saladoid diagnostics.

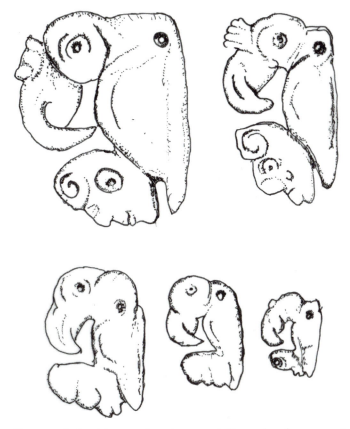

Figure 3.6. Lapidary carvings in green jadite and amber serpentine from the site of La Hueca, Vieques (after Chanlatte and Narganes 2005:22). The largest artifact is 57 mm tall.

When all of these Huecoid-related sites are considered together, three important things must be acknowledged about the sites in which Huecoid material is found in isolation from WOR ceramics. First, the people who lived at La Hueca and similar sites cannot possibly be viewed as a group that preceded Saladoid people into the Caribbean and then disappeared or were on the way to disappearing during the early Saladoid (in Puerto Rico, during Hacienda Grande times). In other words, they were not an advance guard. The charcoal dates from Punta Candelero span more than 1,000 years (see Figure 3.7), from around cal 250 B.C. until after cal A.D. 1000

(Rodríguez 1989:table 1). A similarly long sequence has been documented at La Hueca, and it is also quite well dated through the first millennium and into the second millennium A.D. Indeed in the "New Extension" excavations of Block Z, a region of the site that has only Huecoid-style ceramics, dates from about cal A.D. 1050 until after the time of the European conquest or after (Narganes 1991). Following Oliver (1998:271) I agree that we cannot ignore this persuasive evidence for a very long-term occupation at La Hueca and Punta Candelero and must fundamentally reassess what it means for Caribbean prehistory.

Second, it is now clear that Huecoid and Saladoid sites existed side by side for long periods. The site of Sorcé is immediately adjacent to La Hueca and has a more conventional Saladoid date range of cal 100 B.C. to cal A.D. 700 (Narganes 1991; Oliver 1998), as well as a general style of WOR pottery decoration comparable to the bulk of contemporary Saladoid sites. Based on the radiocarbon chronology for the sites, both sites were occupied for all that time. Punta Candelero also has adjacent non-Huecoid components. Third, it must be acknowledged that there are significant differences between the Huecoid and the Saladoid artifacts, differences that may have deeper cultural and historical ramifications than ceramic decorative modes might suggest. One important area of research on this is the lithic analysis done by Reniel Rodríguez Ramos (2001) on the sites of La Hueca and Sorcé and on both the Huecoid and Saladoid (Cuevas period) components of Punta Candelero. He concluded that there were identifiable differences between the lithic assemblages of the Huecoid and Saladoid sites (Rodríguez Ramos 2001:178–88). He saw differences in the raw material that was used and differences in the way that raw material – in the form of cores of nodules of chert – was turned into usable tools. Chert was far more prevalent in the Huecoid components. It was difficult to establish comparability in units but in general the Huecoid components had three to eight times as much chert by weight per excavated meter than the Saladoid components. The Huecoid reduction strategy, which aimed to produce flakes from discoidal cores, was different from the rather haphazard Saladoid approach, and it left different kinds of cores. Within the ground stone assemblages, the most common tool – the biconvex celt – is found in both components, but the Saladoid

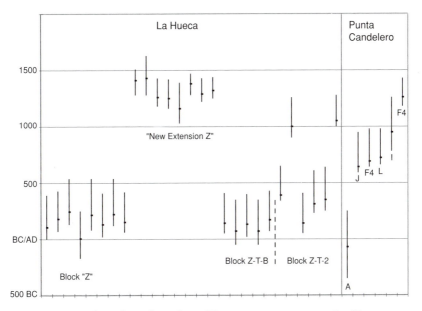

Figure 3.7. Radiocarbon dates from Huecan components at La Hueca and Punta Candelero, showing calibrated 2-sigma ranges of dates based on charcoal in Oliver (1998:tables 18.1 and 18.2).

deposits had ground stone tool types absent in the Huecoid deposits and vice versa (Rodríguez Ramos 2001:144–74, 183–7). In sum, the lithics from these two kinds of sites were related in some ways, yet clearly distinct.

Another very significant point about Rodríguez Ramos's work that will be discussed in more detail shortly is that there are similarities and continuities between the Huecoid lithics and those of the Archaic people who were inhabiting the Caribbean at the time of the early Saladoid occupations.

It is increasingly clear from recent research that La Hueca and Punta Candelero, and probably others, are distinct and special communities, different in material and cultural senses from the broader Saladoid community that surrounded them. As noted, that distinctiveness was very long lived. Given that, one might be tempted to see the Huecoid community as isolationist, rejecting the surrounding mainstream, in a manner analogous to the Amish. The Amish, Mennonites, and other groups of "Plain People" have advocated a separation from the modern world since the inception of the Anabaptist movement in the early 1500s, following the biblical mandate, "Be not conformed to this world" (Romans 12:2). In places like Lancaster County, Pennsylvania, in the United States, the technology and material culture used by Plain People are quite distinct from those of their secular neighbors and would appear so archaeologically if their settlements were excavated. Similarly, some groups of Hasidic Jews maintain group identity and observe scriptural law in ways that mark them as culturally distinct. To some degree this distinction would also register archaeologically. These analogies might be completely inapplicable, but it is difficult to resist searching for some similar historical situation that might be comparable.

In Caribbean prehistory, however, the analogy of a cultural or religious minority within a substantially different mainstream culture is not entirely applicable. In Saladoid times, the artifacts related to the Huecoid phenomenon – ZIC ceramics – are found as a minority constituent of nearly every contemporaneous ceramic assemblage, and they continue to be present for nearly 1,000 years. Clearly there was some relationship between the people at Huecoid sites and the others. Perhaps a better analogy can be seen in monastic communities such as Buddhist monasteries or the monastic orders with the Catholic or Greek Orthodox churches. Religious communities such as these share some characteristics with sites such as La Hueca and Punta Candelero: they are distinct from, but embedded in, a cultural matrix to which they are related. Their distinctive artifacts, symbolically rich and sometimes nonutilitarian, are found in the dominant culture as minority constituents. And although they share many material traits with surrounding people they are distinct and identifiable. Among the distinctions is a markedly greater prevalence in the Huecoid sites of artifacts related to shamanistic hallucination or trance rituals (for example, small zoomorphic grinding stones and pestles). These special-purpose artifacts are used for inhaling consciousness-altering powders or smoke or drinking special drinks and are clearly related to the cohoba rituals of the historic Taíno (Rodríguez 1997:85–6). These practices also related to divination and communication with supernatural beings.

Envisioning La Hueca and Punta Candelero as cultural enclaves, perhaps with religious functions and certainly very long lasting, runs counter to a view of Caribbean prehistory that sees large periods of cultural homogeneity as the norm. It fits better with a view of the Caribbean, during most of its prehistory and in historic times, as a relatively stable mosaic of cultural difference. Whether we imagine them as enclaves with special social functions or persistent cultural isolates involves great speculation on our part. Clearly the Huecoid phenomenon is one of the most interesting topics in Caribbean prehistory and an exciting area for continued research.

SALADOID PEOPLE AND THEIR INTERACTIONS WITH OTHERS

Apart from the relationship between the Huecoid and Saladoid people just discussed, and other internal complexities of Saladoid society, there were several other important groups they interacted with.

The most important of these were the Archaic people whom the Saladoid joined in the Caribbean. As noted in Chapter 2, the Archaic people in the Antilles had two principal areas of origin, one in Central America and one from South America via the Lesser Antilles. These two groups had met and interacted in the territory between western Puerto Rico and Antigua for more than 1,000 years before the Saladoid people arrived and no doubt in that time had diverged into many regional groups, specializing in different areas of the Caribbean.

Saladoid migrants from the Orinoco moved up into regions that the Archaic people had long occupied, and apparently early Saladoid settlement patterns reflect this. Higher islands seem to have been selected over lower ones and places such as the island of Antigua, strongly favored for Archaic settlement, were avoided at first. Early Saladoid settlements were often situated in places with good views, on the windward sides of islands (although this generalization may mask a great deal of variability in locations). Some early sites, such as Hope Estate on St. Martin, seem almost hidden from view from the coast or sea. It would not be hard to imagine that some tensions developed between these two populations, but it does not show up in the archaeological record as it often does in more violent confrontations – as defensive architecture, armaments, or characteristic patterns of injuries in the burial population (Carmine 1997; Lambert 2000).

There is some evidence for cultural interaction or "transculturation" between Archaic and later people. At the Huecoid sites of Punta Candelero and La Hueca, Reniel Rodríguez found continuities between Archaic and Huecoid use of lithics. The characteristic "edge grinders" or edge-ground cobbles that were probably important in processing plant materials continued in the Huecoid sites. These artifacts, and round, pitted stones, are also found in some early Saladoid (Hacienda Grande period, in the Puerto Rican ceramic sequence) sites. The degree of technological interaction seems to vary among the early sites. As Rodríguez Ramos notes,

> ...the [Huecoid] context of Punta Candelero seems more "Archaic-like" in its technological emphasis than that from La Hueca site. The greater emphasis on freehand flaking and other overall unmeasurable qualities in that artifactual repertoire, make us estimate that the [Huecoid] occupation of Punta Candelero is earlier than that of La Hueca site, as is also reflected by the radiocarbon dates collected from these sites. Also, the lithic remains seem to reinforce Haviser's (1991) argument that the [Huecoid] materials [from the] La Hueca site presents a higher degree of Saladoid influence when compared to other Early Ceramic contexts such as that from Hope Estate.

Rodríguez cautions that some of these ideas are speculative and must be evaluated with future research, but they are certainly plausible if one envisions the early Saladoid period as one of multiple interacting cultural groups.

At the site of Hacienda Grande, Rouse and Alegría (1990:66) found similar "hammer-grinders" and "edge-grinders" that might be the result of mixed deposits, but they could be evidence of Saladoid people adopting the tools from people who had lived there a long time (1990:20–5). Walker (1985:186, 190–1) and others are convinced of the edge-grinding tool's continuity from Archaic to Saladoid times. If these tools were involved in processing vegetable foods, as can be inferred from their use-wear, they may indicate the transfer of local knowledge and ways of adapting to the Caribbean environment from one group to the other, if not the interaction and fusion of the two in a longer term cultural sense.

A very important example of the possible interaction of Saladoid and Archaic people occurs in eastern Dominican Republic. Marcio Veloz Maggiolo, Elpidio Ortega, Plinio Pina, and others from the Museo del Hombre Dominicano excavated the site during a period of widespread and intensive archaeological research in the Dominican Republic in the 1960s and 1970s. In their 1976 publication Ortega and his colleagues noted, "The site of El Caimito was worked for the first time in 1972, and it was considered to be preceramic since it produced a radiocarbon date of 15 B.C. . . ." (Ortega, Veloz Maggiolo, and Pina Peña 1976:276). When they discovered ceramics they returned to the site for a more extensive program of field work and excavated most of a small mound. Four radiocarbon dates yielded a range from cal 390 B.C. to cal A.D. 410. Apart from the ceramics, they found a range of artifacts that would be typical of Archaic period sites – flake tools, edge-grinders or martillos, manos, metates, and mortars, and fragments of petaloid axes. The excavators did not find cassava griddles among the ceramics, and the faunal and botanical analyses conducted suggested a dependence on collecting wild foods and the possible absence of cultivation, at least cultivation or domestication on a large scale (Ortega *et al.* 1976:280).

In the 1970s Caribbean archaeologists in general were paying a great deal of attention to the sequence of prehistoric migrations and their impact on the archipelago (Keegan 2000). Initially, El Caimito was interpreted from the widely held perspective that different kinds of assemblages usually meant different migrations from the mainland. Ortega *et al.* (1976:280) concluded that "El Caimito showed that non-'Saladoid' groups arrived in the Greater Antilles area at the same time or before the Saladoid groups, and made or acquired ceramics of good quality." Alberta Zucci and Kay Tarble also related the El Caimito ceramics to some material at the site of Agüerito in the Middle Orinoco (Zucci and Tarble 1984). Indeed, the site may still prove to be evidence for an exploratory foray into the Caribbean by that or some unknown group from the mainland.

In recent years, however, other explanations apart from migration have received wider consideration in the Caribbean. Luis Chanlatte, William Keegan, Irving Rouse, Marcio Veloz Maggiolo, and others have assigned greater importance to processes of cultural interaction going on in place within the Caribbean. From that perspective,

El Caimito could be interpreted as a manifestation of the interaction of Archaic people with Saladoid and Huecoid people, which was what was going on in the eastern Greater Antilles and particularly in areas such as eastern Dominican Republic. The appearance of typically Archaic implements in Huecoid and Hacienda Grande sites in Puerto Rico and Vieques suggests a transfer of both technology and of adaptive strategies. El Caimito probably shows a similar adoption of a Saladoid or Huecoid technology – pottery making – by the people who had lived in the Greater Antilles so successfully for so long. In that interaction it was the Saladoid people who had the most to gain, because over millennia the Archaic people had developed sophisticated knowledge about the land and resources, climate, possibilities, and dangers in the islands.

It is also possible El Caimito and other comparable sites (see Keegan 2006 for a discussion of these) represent the independent invention of ceramics in the Greater Antilles. Rodríguez Ramos (2001) has suggested the term *Pre-Arawak Pottery Horizon* to refer to Archaic sites with pottery that predate any possible Saladoid contact. As Keegan (2006) concludes, "the presence of pottery in pre-Saladoid and pre-Ostionoid Archaic contexts can no longer be denied. Dozen of sites that contain a largely Archaic tool kit and varying quantities of pottery have been identified from Cuba to the northern Lesser Antilles, and the sites date to as early as 2600 BC. Although most of the early sites contain very few potsherds, the frequency of pottery in otherwise Archaic sites increased through time."

In some ways the pottery of El Caimito is strongly reminiscent of later pottery on the island of Hispaniola, especially that known as Meillacan, the most widespread pottery on the island (Rouse 1992:92–101; Veloz Maggiolo, Ortega, and Caba Fuentes 1981). Its decorations include parallel line incision and, like some of the pottery associated with the historic Taíno, incisions ending in punctations. In some ways both the El Caimito pottery and the Meillacan, with their areas of parallel incised lines patterned at perpendicularly to each other, and occasional basketweave applique, seem intentionally to evoke the decoration of baskets made of organic materials (Figure 3.8; see also Veloz Maggiolo *et al.* 1981). It is as if the

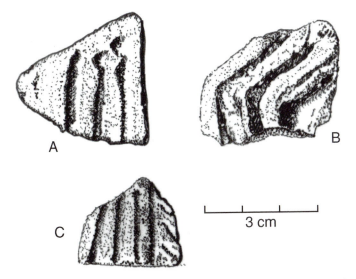

Figure 3.8. Sherds from the site of El Caimito (after Ortega *et al.* 1976).

material technology of ceramics was adopted based on Saladoid or other models, but to a large extent the potters' decisions about decorative treatment were based on existing basketry rather than Saladoid decorative modes. This preference was not exclusive, however, because some early Hispaniolan pottery does follow Saladoid pottery in stylistic motifs and execution (Veloz Maggiolo 1972: 308–11). As discussed in Chapter 4, Meillacan pottery clearly has strong continuities with Archaic material culture, and El Caimito is very likely the earliest known example of the process of cultural interaction that gave rise to it.

SALADOID LIFE IN THE LESSER AND GREATER ANTILLES

The Economy of the Saladoid Migrants

By the time the Saladoid people moved into the Caribbean, and for several thousand years before that on the mainland, they had been living in permanent villages and subsisting in part on domesticated plants. Their economy was adapted through hundreds of human generations of refinements to the riverine and coastal environments of what are now Venezuela, Guyana, Surinam, and French Guiana (Boomert 2000). From these environments they made use of hundreds of species of plants, both wild and domesticated. They also hunted, fished, and collected a wide range of animals, from large mammals such as deer and tapirs to shellfish and crabs. Apart from using plants and animals for food, the mainland ancestors of the Saladoid people who came to the Caribbean also used the forest resources for medicines, adornment, and nearly every part of their material culture. As with the Archaic people who preceded them into the Caribbean, more than 95% of their material culture was made of perishable materials (Newsom and Wing 2004).

The main plant in their horticultural system was manioc (*Manihot esculenta*, also called cassava and yuca), a root crop that was a good source of carbohydrates and calories (Newsom and Wing 2004; Piperno and Pearsall 1998). Manioc is a staple throughout much of the lowland tropics, and there are hundreds of different kinds. They can be roughly divided into "sweet" and "bitter" varieties, depending on their levels of toxicity. Without careful processing, compounds in raw manioc break down into hydrocyanic acid, which is poisonous. Sweet manioc can be processed fairly easily whereby the toxins are eliminated through cooking. Bitter manioc receives more elaborate treatment, involving peeling, grating, washing, straining of the mash, drying, and ultimately cooking into large, thin cakes. Part of the rationale for this process is to eliminate the hydrocyanic acid, but it also turns the manioc, which cannot be stored for long once dug out of the ground, into a flour that can be stored. The rhythms and demands of processing manioc structure the lives of many in the region. Well-drained fields must be cleared and planted, and the roots take between 6 and 18 months to mature, depending on the variety. Soil fertility declines under manioc cultivation and when it is possible people will move their gardens after a few years, clearing another patch of river terrace and letting the old ones be taken over again by the forest (Newsom and Wing 2004).

Manioc has a special place in the world of the Saladoid people and their descendants in the Caribbean, as the primary staple plant it does in most horticultural societies. But it was far from the only crop they grew. As in much of the Americas, maize, beans, and squashes were probably significant domesticates, and chili peppers, in their vast range of forms from small to large and mild tasting to explosive, were also a part of the South American cuisine taken to the Antilles (Newsom 1993; Newsom and Wing 2004). Some of the many fruits that were in use by the historic Indians of the Caribbean may have been native to the islands, and others were brought from the mainland. Most of these are still common plants in the West Indies and demonstrate the considerable extent to which indigenous knowledge and lifeways have survived into the present. For most of these there are many and varied common names and spellings, but some of the most common are mamey apple (*Mammea americana*), custard apple (*Annona reticulata*), soursop (*Annona muricata*), guava (*Psidium guajava*), papaya (*Carica papaya*), pineapple (*Ananas comosus*), avocado (*Persea americana*), and passion fruit (*Passiflora edulis*).

The archaeological evidence from the Saladoid period is not complete enough to claim with confidence that all of these plants were taken to the Caribbean Saladoid times. There is, however, enough evidence to conclude that the lowland South American economy transported to the Antilles by the Saladoid people (and probably to some extent by their Archaic predecessors as well) was rich and varied. Even among the root crops they had a dozen other alternatives to the many kinds of manioc they grew (Boomert 2000:97). With the addition of all of the kinds of wild plant foods to be had in the islands, and the wealth of marine and terrestrial animals, they had an extremely productive economy.

To summarize, the ancestors of the Saladoid people had developed a complex food production system of over millennia on the lowland rivers and coasts of northeast South America and from there they brought it into the Caribbean. Over time they adapted this economic system to the island environments, adding endemic plants and animals to their list of useful species and learning the different climatic rhythms of the islands. After an initial period of exploration and probably frequent movement, Saladoid settlements became very stable, with sites being occupied continuously for centuries with little change in their size (Siegel 1989). Many other features of Saladoid cultural life also show a similar conservatism. The consistent use of some iconographic motifs in Saladoid pottery and other media over time reflects a cosmology and worldview that was slow to change, and many elements of this cultural system of symbols and shared meanings persist as part of Taíno culture. Much of our understanding of Saladoid cosmology comes from their pottery and other media such as carved precious stone and shell. Recently a great deal of new insight has been gained through the archaeological exploration of Saladoid houses and village layouts. It is there we will begin, before turning to pottery and other forms of cultural expression.

SALADOID HOUSES AND VILLAGES

A remarkable change in archaeologists' vision of Saladoid life began in the 1980s with the large-area excavation of substantial parts of Saladoid villages. This was done at the site of Golden Rock on St. Eustatius, Maisabel in northern Puerto Rico, Punta Candelero in southeastern Puerto Rico, Tibes in southern Puerto Rico, Tutu village on St. Thomas, and Trants on Montserrat and on smaller scales at several other sites. (For later periods this kind of excavation strategy was also employed by Kathy Deagan at En Bas Saline in Haiti.) Aad Versteeg's research at Golden Rock from 1984 to 1988 was a pioneering example of this research strategy. Before this project the majority of archaeological explorations of Saladoid sites focused on stratified midden deposits, where over time trash and food remains had accumulated. In these middens pottery, lithic tools, and nearly all classes of artifacts could be recovered in the greatest numbers with the least amount of excavation. That kind of concentrated block excavation was essential in reconstructing a chronological sequence of occupations and in discerning changes in artifact type and frequency through time. Indeed the overall chronology of Caribbean prehistory was largely based on this sort of concentrated excavation strategy. Apart from occasional postmolds, however, archaeologists encountered very few remnants of the Saladoid people's built environment – the houses they lived in and the other structures they built and used in their settlements. Many archaeologists prior to these research projects (and I speak from personal experience) tended to see trash middens as the most significant indicators of the presence of archaeological sites, without a clear concept of how these middens related to the houses, plazas, and activity areas that were so revealing about the lives of the people who lived there.

At Golden Rock, Versteeg excavated a great deal of the midden deposits but also used mechanized equipment to remove the overburden from 2,800 sq m of the village. The area had been in cultivation for centuries and the material that was removed had probably been plowed dozens if not hundreds of times. What was revealed by this procedure was a stratum of light-colored soil that would have been slightly below the village's ground surface when it was occupied. Careful scraping revealed hundreds of soil stains where posts or pits or other features had penetrated the original surface and cut through the light soil below. These features, large and small, were strewn across the site's surface, and could be connected in connect-the-dots fashion into any number of patterns of houses, large and small. Each feature was excavated by slicing it down the middle from top to bottom, revealing in profile its depth and shape. When postmolds of similar depth and profile were compared, the layout of individual houses became apparent (Figure 3.9) (Versteeg 1987; Versteeg and Schinkel 1992).

Versteeg and his colleagues found houses dating to two periods at Golden Rock. Three smaller houses, about 7 m in diameter, date to the fifth century A.D. The posts of these structures are shown on Figure 3.9 as unfilled circles connected by dotted lines. The earlier houses are spaced about 20 m apart and may have been occupied at the same time. Two of the houses from the later period, dating into the ninth century A.D., are built in the same spots as two of the houses from the earlier period, and there is other archaeological evidence for continuity of occupation between the two building phases. The later houses, shown on Figure 3.8 as filled circles connected with solid lines, are about 20 m in diameter and are more robustly built than the earlier structures. The pattern of large posts, sunk nearly 2 m into the ground, shows strong similarities to historically known communal houses used in lowland South America

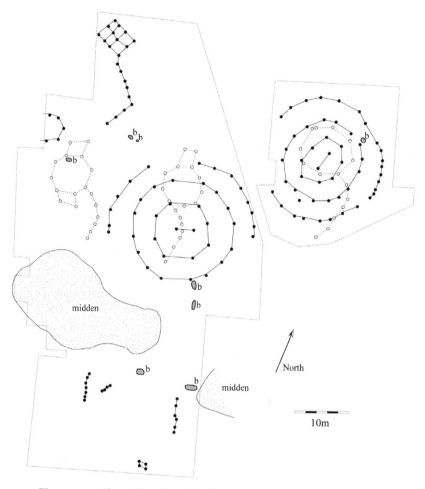

Figure 3.9. Plan of the site of Golden Rock on St. Eustatius (after Versteeg and Schinkel 1992).

(Figure 3.9). These houses are conical in shape and nearly 20 m tall. The major timbers were tied together with a framework of smaller poles and the whole exterior was thatched (Figure 3.10). The patterns of post molds also suggest that there were attached or free-standing walls away from the structures. These are interpreted as windbreaks or screens, creating areas on the leeward side sheltered from the prevailing east wind and to some degree segregated from the rest of the settlement.

Figure 3.10. A late-twentieth-century Maloca from lowland South America.

The northern part of the excavated area seems to be an area of ceremonial importance. There are several caches of artifacts and burials in this area and a rectangular structure, also with an associated windbreak. Because of its association with the caches and burials, and again through comparison with ethnographic information from South America, the rectangular structure is seen as having a cere- monial function, perhaps as a men's house (Versteeg 1987; Versteeg and Schinkel 1992).

The large area excavation carried out at Golden Rock by Versteeg and the University of Leiden team revealed a settlement of large houses that was probably occupied continuously for 500 years. Even so it is only part of the site. Other parts of the site were either destroyed or paved over during the building of St. Eustatius's air- port. Josselin deJong's map from 1947 shows a cluster of five mid- dens occupying an area that is about 500 m in diameter. Several other houses were almost certainly associated with these middens. As has been noted, Golden Rock was occupied relatively late in Saladoid times. Other sites in the Leeward Islands preceded it by many centuries. It was also not unusual for its size or architecture but is important precisely because it is probably unexceptional and representative of a great number of late Saladoid sites in the Lesser Antilles and Puerto Rico.

SALADOID SOCIAL AND POLITICAL ORGANIZATION

The spatial organization of settlements, including the spatial relationship of central spaces, special buildings, and burial areas, yields
information on many other aspects of Saladoid life. The spatial relationships of buildings and other features help inform us about indigenous social organization, conventions about residence and inheri-
tance, and patterns of social inequality.

At Golden Rock, on St. Eustatius, most of the burials were located
in the central plaza. This is the case at most Saladoid sites. Although
the pattern is not completely clear, it seems that the practice is
even more common on Puerto Rico. There, three well-excavated
sites show the same pattern and yield evidence about its possible
meaning and important changes that occurred at the end of the
Saladoid period, about A.D. 600.

The site of Maisabel is on the north-central coast of Puerto Rico,
about 30 miles west of San Juan. It is on the island's rich coastal plain,
in an area with many lagoons and wetlands. It is right on the coast
on a low rise of less than 10 m, about 1 km from the mouth of the
Río Cibuco. The site dates from early Saladoid times and continues
into the Ostionoid period (from a few centuries B.C. until around
A.D. 1000). Like most sites containing the impressive white-on-red
Saladoid ceramics and lapidary work, the site was known to local
artifact collectors. A few archaeologists, including Ovidio Dávila
and Peter Roe, had carried out excavations at Maisabel in the late
1970s and 1980s. Peter Siegel and the Centro de Investigaciones
Indígenas de Puerto Rico led extensive excavations in the mid- and
late 1980s (Siegel 1989, 1992).

In the Maisabel site's original, early Saladoid configuration, it was
a circular village with houses and mounded middens surrounding a
ceremonial complex and cemetery (Siegel 1992:188–91). Throughout the site's long occupation, the cemetery remained a constant
feature at the center of the site. Siegel concluded that "the overall
village layout of Maisabel can be interpreted from the perspective
of South Amerindian lowland cosmology. The central sacred space
(cemetery ringed by the mounded middens) provided a focal point,
around which daily and ritual life revolved, spatially and temporally.

Perhaps this area also served as a plaza" (Siegel 1992:190). Burial practices changed though time at Maisabel, as later people chose to bury most of their dead inside their large communal houses. A few individuals were still buried in the central cemetery, however.

A similar shift in burial patterns – from a centrally placed cemetery to a practice of burying the dead in surrounding houses – may be seen at the site of Tibes, along the Río Portugués near the modern city of Ponce on Puerto Rico's southern coastal plain. Tibes is remarkable for its early examples of ceremonial precincts lined with stone borders or pavements. These are the predecessors of the stone or slab-lined "ball courts" or *bateyes* of later prehistory and the period of European contact (Alegría 1983). The site is also very important because it was occupied continuously from at least A.D. 400–1200 and shows a transition from a typical Saladoid site to what is arguably the Caribbean's first "chiefdom" or ranked society at about A.D. 900–1200 (Curet and Oliver 1998:224; Veloz Maggiolo 1991). Antonio Curet, Lee Newsom, and a team of researchers from the Field Museum of Natural History and Penn State University have been working at Tibes since the mid-1990s, building on the earlier work of Alvarado Zayas and González Colón. Their research has revealed a sequence of the development of the site that is similar to that found at Maisabel. Again there is a ring of middens with a central cleared space in the center. There were two clusters of Saladoid burials within the central space, one in what was to become the largest ceremonial precinct of the site and another under another stone-demarcated feature or ball court (Curet and Rodríguez Gracia 1995). Once the plazas were constructed, the people at Tibes tended to bury their dead in association with houses or midden areas, as they had at Maisabel.

At Tibes and similar sites the reuse of the cemetery area as a ceremonial space was clearly not a coincidence. These areas continued to be important to the community but in a transformed way. Curet and Oliver (1998:230–1) argue that this marks an important change in Caribbean social organization. The earlier practices of using central cemeteries, they argue, "were instituted, in part, to legitimize both the extended, kin-based corporate groups that controlled rights over the resources within their territory and the ideology to perpetuate

them." They further argue that "in post-Saladoid times the corporate group had been replaced by an elite group or household
that was to assert control over and manage the critical, ideological,
and symbolic resources that were once in the hands of communal
institutions." This may well be the case, particularly at a site such as
Tibes, with early evidence for the development of social complexity.
At smaller sites, the replacement of Saladoid cemeteries with central
plazas and the transition to burying people in domestic contexts may
reflect a shift in the way people understood and represented their
identities – a move from identifying with a single cohesive community to seeing oneself as a member of one or another distinct lineage
or kinship groups.

These changes in burial patterns and community organization are
related to a broad set of transformations beginning to take place by
around A.D. 600. Beginning at this time, and continuing until the
time of the European conquest of the Greater Antilles, new and more
complex forms of social and political organization emerged in the
Caribbean. These developments will be explored in the following
chapters.

CHAPTER 4

THE TAÍNO

At the end of the Saladoid period, the Caribbean world was changing quickly. Populations were growing from one end of the archipelago to the other; people were moving into areas that had been uninhabited or sparsely populated. Between A.D. 600 and 1200, a process of elaboration of social and political organization was underway, ultimately resulting in the complex Taíno polities observed by European explorers. All of these things were happening unevenly, however, with rapid and dramatic change in some areas balanced by continuity and relatively slow change in others.

This chapter explores the processes of change that were taking place, with emphasis on several themes: the emergence of social and political complexity, the diversity of Caribbean societies as they developed in different contexts, and the importance of the interactions of people with different histories and cultures – on one hand, the descendants of the Archaic people, with over 4,000 years of history living in the Greater Antilles, and, on the other, the descendants of the Saladoid people, with relatively closer ties to the South American mainland. It also deals with the growing significance of interactions between the Greater and Lesser Antilles in the last few centuries before European contact. Exciting changes were taking places in both regions, and events in any part of the archipelago had a wider impact than had ever been seen before.

The timing of the transition that took place at the end of the Saladoid period was varied. After A.D. 600 modes of pottery decoration changed quickly in Puerto Rico and adjacent islands as the Cuevas style of Saladoid ceramics was replaced by the Monserrate style (Curet 1997). In other places, however, such as the northern Lesser Antilles, polychrome pottery clearly related to Saladoid ceramics continued nearly unchanged until at least A.D. 850 or 900 (Hofman 1993; Versteeg 1987). In fact in much of the Lesser Antilles, the period from A.D. 600 to at least A.D. 900 showed very little in the way of dramatic change in archaeological remains. However, interaction and cultural change were intensifying in western Puerto Rico and eastern Dominican Republic, with profound changes appearing on the western side of the Mona Passage (between Puerto Rico and Hispaniola). In all of Puerto Rico and Hispaniola, this was a time of major change, marked by the appearance of ceremonial centers and other evidence of complex society.

In eastern Hispaniola, fully sedentary villages based on horticulture became the dominant form of settlement. This change was evidenced by the widespread appearance of red-painted Ostionoid pottery similar to that used in Puerto Rico. That link may lend itself to an interpretation that this pottery represents a new migration of people, but we should be cautious in making this assumption. As noted in Chapters 2 and 3, some people in eastern Dominican Republic had been making pottery since the last centuries B.C., for instance, at the site of El Caimito, and they had probably been cultivating domesticated plants for a long time as well.

In trying to understand this period of change and population movement in Hispaniola and further west, we have to rely to a large extent on the pottery that survives on archaeological sites. In the preceding discussion a series of ceramics called Ostionoid was mentioned, and this group contains three component subseries – Ostionan, Meillacan, and Chican (Rouse 1992). These subseries, their local variants, and the stages of transformation the ceramic assemblages undergo through time, are the biggest part of the evidence with which to attempt to reconstruct this complicated period of population movement and culture change.

Using Rouse's terminology, the Ostionan Ostionoid ceramics retain a lot of the characteristics of the late Saladoid ceramics from which they derive. Vessel forms include straight-sided bowls instead of the bell-shaped Saladoid bowls. De Wolf (1953:33) succinctly

5 cm

Figure 4.1. Mellacoide sherds from the Río Verde Phase in La Vega, Dominican Republic. After Veloz Maggiolo *et al.* (1981:221).

describes the "redware" pottery of Jamaica and captures the main characteristics of Ostionan Ostionoid ceramics. They are, he said,

> Medium fine grained but poorly fired; color, reds, tans and greys; average thickness 0.5 cm; shape, open bowls with some flat bottoms; shoulder, straight or incurving; rim, tapered to the lip; lip, rounded or flat; D-shaped handles, amorphous and tab lugs; some painting and rubbing of restricted areas.

Meillacan ceramics have many of the same forms but with more incurving bowls. They did not choose to paint their pots red except in the earliest Meillacan sites (Veloz Maggiolo *et al.* 1981:307–12), and they developed a rougher exterior, often with rectilinear incision or the applied decorations illustrated in Figure 4.1. Some of these seem to give ceramic vessels the textural characteristics of woven baskets, perhaps echoing in clay the forms and designs that had formerly been made of perishable materials. In addition, some of the

Figure 4.2. Late prehistoric ceramics from the Dominican Republic (after Veloz Maggiolo 1972:plates 18 and 25).

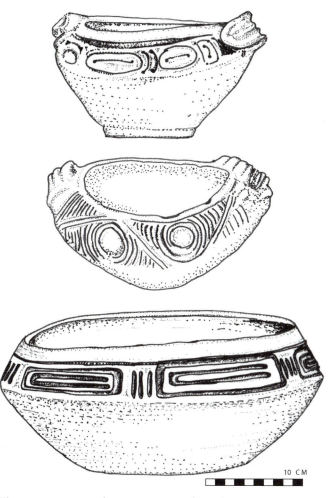

Figure 4.3. Late prehistoric ceramics from the Dominican Republic (after Veloz Maggiolo 1972:plates 14 and 26).

shoulders of the vessels were decorated with patterns of punctations, which also appear to copy the patterns of baskets.

In Chican Ostionoid pottery, red painting is almost completely absent (but is occasionally used in Puerto Rico), along with strap and D-shaped handles. Potters paid a great deal of attention to deeply incised decoration on the shoulders of the mostly incurving vessels and modeled intricate, sculptural lugs (Figures 4.2 and 4.3). Whole complex vessels are decorated with this modeled incision, sometimes with modeled faces on the handles or elaborate spouts of bottles. Effigy vessels are an important constituent of Chican ceramic art (Kerchache 1994; Veloz Maggiolo 1972).

Rouse (1992:92–9) and others have interpreted the spread of Ostionoid ceramics into Hispaniola and the western Greater Antilles and Bahamas as a migration. Rouse (1992:96) argues that "[T]he Ostionan expansion was obviously a population movement, for it resulted in the displacement of the previous Casimiran population. Jamaica may be an exception; because no Casimiroid remains have been found there, the Ostionans would appear to have been the original settlers of that island."

In Hispaniola, however, one regional variant of the Ostionan series of ceramics – the Meillacan or Mellacoide – seems markedly different from other kinds. In *Los Modos de Vida Mellacoides* (1981:309–10), Marcio Veloz Maggiolo, Elpidio Ortega, and Angel Caba Fuentes comment,

> It is evident that [the Mellacoides] do not appear, from the point of view of ceramic decorations, to have precedents either in the island of Santo Domingo nor in the Antilles, in contrast with the Ostionoid ceramics which appear to result from Saladoid forms, or as can be seen with the Chicoid ceramics whose decorative patterns are present in Saladoid and Barrancoid pottery from eastern Venezuela.

In other words, the Ostionoid migrants from Puerto Rico underwent some sort of change in the Cibao Valley of the Dominican Republic and began making a new kind of pottery. The regional pottery variant there, the Meillacan or Mellacoide, exhibited design elements that could not be traced to Saladoid forms. Veloz Maggiolo *et al.* were forced to look outside the Greater Antilles for this influence:

> Not having evidence for local evolution, nor connecting archaeological evidence in all of the Antillean arc, we must suppose that the Mellacoide ceramics are the result of a prehistoric migration that came into the island of Santo Domingo and affixed their decorative patterns on to a well elaborated Ostionoid ceramic

medium – that which was the product of farmers with seg-
mentary organization who accepted the fusion of a new ethnic group, generating a rapid change in their settlement pattern and conception of the environment. (Veloz Maggiolo *et al.*
1981:309–10)

In the nearly 25 years since that was written, evidence has not
accumulated for such a migration to the Caribbean. Also, in recent
years Veloz Maggiolo and Rouse have placed more emphasis on the
importance of processes of interaction and transculturation between
the long-established inhabitants of Hispaniola and their long-time
neighbors, and both scholars have proposed another theory regard-
ing this question. That solution, which is favored here, is that the
substantial changes reflected in Mellacoide ceramics, such as other
technology, settlement patterns, and economy, are evidence for the
cultural synthesis of Ostionoid people and ideas with the Archaic
people who had been living on Hispaniola for over 4,000 years. The
Mellacoide people reflect the integration of Archaic and Ostionoid
peoples, and their way of life retains a great deal of the Archaic
relationship with the land. At a great many of the Meillacan sites
investigated by Veloz Maggiolo *et al.* (1981), the Mellacoide ceramics
are found in use alongside the lithics and ground stone implements
characteristic of the Casimiroid series.

Although it is clear that some migration took place, because
heretofore uninhabited areas were colonized, there is also evidence
to suggest that this transformation was less the continuation of a
Saladoid migratory wave and more a reflection of the adoption
of elements of the Ostionoid economy and material culture by
the descendants of Archaic people living in Hispaniola. Keegan
(2000:150) has argued that the idea of pottery making had come
to Hispaniola as early as 350 B.C., and rapid spread of Ostionan
and later Meillacan ceramics reflected a "hybridization of Archaic
and Saladoid cultures." Rouse (1992:97–8) also discusses the possibility that cultural interaction played a role in the emergence of
later groups when discussing the Meillacan ceramic subseries: "Local
Courians [the Archaic groups living there before these events] possibly became assimilated into the invading Ostionan population and

caused the change from Ostionan to Meillac pottery." More work on this interesting period is needed, but it now seems likely that through many centuries of living side by side in eastern Hispaniola, and perhaps trading across the passage between there and Puerto Rico, a new cultural identity was emerging, and it probably included the biological descendants of both Saladoid and Archaic people.

As we have seen before in Caribbean prehistory, the long-term interaction of groups of people with different cultures and histories appears to have acted as a catalyst for change. In Hispaniola it led to substantial population growth, significant shifts in the way food was produced, and ultimately to social and political change. All of these things led to new migrations into the Bahamas and Jamaica, and the spread of sedentary village life and new modes of food production westward into Cuba.

THE COLONIZATION OF JAMAICA, THE BAHAMAS, AND CUBA

Whatever the balance was between population movement and local cultural change on the island of Hispaniola, significant changes were taking place between A.D. 600 and 1000. Some of the clearest evidence for this is the colonization of Jamaica and the Bahamas apparently for the first time, and the spread of the Ostionoid archaeological assemblage into eastern Cuba. Very likely all three of these movements involved the migration of people from Hispaniola into those islands.

As far as is known, Jamaica had not been occupied by humans prior to A.D. 600 or later. It is quite remarkable that such a large land mass in the Americas went uncolonized for so long. It may be that evidence of earlier occupations or at least visits will eventually come to light, for Jamaica is just beginning to receive the intensity of archaeological research that the other Greater Antillean islands have experienced. The earliest sites appear to date to A.D. 650 or so, although there are some slightly earlier dates that may push colonization back to between A.D. 600 and 700 (Lee 1980; Rouse and Allaire 1978:490).

It would have been another extraordinary moment in the human history of the Caribbean to find an uninhabited island as large as Jamaica, 130 km across and 80 km wide. Like the other islands in the Greater Antilles when they were first discovered by humans, Jamaica had several large and relatively defenseless species that became extinct after human colonization (including flightless birds, large rodents, sloths, monkeys, and bats). The colonists also brought with them some of the mammalian species they found useful, such as the agouti and dog.

The coast and interior valleys of Jamaica were eventually densely settled, and the island has a rich and still relatively understudied archaeological record. On Columbus's second voyage, in 1494, Bernáldez described the island as follows:

> It is a very mighty land, and beyond measure populous, so that even on the sea-shore as well as inland, every part is filled with villages and those very large and very near one another, at 4 leagues distance. (Bernáldez, in Jane 1988, II:124)

Bernáldez describes the scene when Columbus and his company first met with the people who had by that time been living on Jamaica for around eight centuries:

> The admiral entered the harbour and anchored, and so many Indians came down to it that they covered the land, and all were painted a thousand colours, but the majority black, and all were naked as is their custom. They wore feathers of various kinds on the head and had the breast and stomach covered with palm leaves. They made the greatest howling in the world and shot darts, although they were out of range. (Bernáldez, in Jane 1988, II:128)

In Jamaica it appears that the earliest explorers and colonists used Ostionan Ostionoid ceramics and thus probably had connections with Puerto Rico and eastern Hispaniola and with others living on southern Hispaniola and Cuba. On Jamaica this pottery is called Redware and is found in sites around the coast. Lee (1980) describes a sample of 11 sites and notes that they were almost always coastal and near a beach, near fresh water, and relatively shallow in depth.

A different kind of ceramic assemblage is found at sites dating to around A.D. 900 and after. This pottery is rougher, thicker, and related to the Meillacan pottery mentioned earlier. In Jamaica it is called White Marl, and after A.D. 900 it is the dominant ceramic assemblage on Jamaica until contact.

The amount of prehistoric archaeological research that has been carried out on Jamaica is less than what has been done on the surrounding islands, and many of the dates we have for sites are single dates without a lot of information on their contexts, so more work needs to be done before we can draw more solid conclusions about the early colonization of the island. On present evidence, however, it seems that the Ostionan Redware was present at the earliest sites, and at some or most of these sites it was not mixed with later Meillacan pottery. Then, a few centuries later, the Meillacan White Marl pottery came into widespread use. Lee (1980:598, 602) suggests a hiatus between these two kinds of sites, seeing the earlier sites as a failed attempt at colonization. He speculates, "[D]id they, perhaps, send scouts ahead to some other location and then pack up to go off to a new and better area? There is no evidence to show that this happened, so perhaps our Redware people were themselves an exploratory group checking out Jamaica on behalf of others who decided not to follow" (Lee 1980:598).

Although the evidence is not yet very good for this period, I think we can imagine this differently: after A.D. 600 or so the relationship between the terminal Saladoid people of Puerto Rico and eastern Hispaniola and the terminal Archaic or Casimiroid people of the rest of Hispaniola changed, and a new culture emerged with elements of both ancestries. Instead of being rather culturally independent neighbors, as they apparently had been for centuries, they became participants in a new hybrid and plural society. In the process they unleashed a dramatic period of new exploration and colonization, as well as rapid population growth. In the centuries between these events and the arrival of the Europeans, the many societies of the Greater Antilles developed or elaborated on their differences, resulting in a good deal of cultural diversity among, say, the people of highland Puerto Rico, Jamaica, and the Bahamas. But they shared a cultural connection that came from the synthesis of Saladoid and

Archaic ancestries. The fundamental cultural connection that come from their dual ancestry may be seen in all of the Greater Antillean societies encountered by European explorers, and it forms a critical part of what it is to be Taíno.

So after A.D. 600 Jamaica became part of the known world to the people of Hispaniola, Cuba, and Puerto Rico (Atkinson 2006). Although the 140-km passage to Cuba and the 180-km passage to Haiti were formidable, the island was from that time onward known and accessible to colonization by a range of groups. The Jamaicans stayed in contact with other Jamaicans and with the rest of the Greater Antillean world by sea. In Bernáldez's account of Columbus's trip to Jamaica, he describes their means of staying connected:

> They have more canoes than in any other part of those regions, and the largest that have yet been seen. . . . In all those parts, every cacique has a great canoe, of which he is proud and which is for his service, as here a caballero prides himself on possessing a great and beautiful ship. So they have them decorated at the bow and stern with metal bands and with paintings, so that their beauty is wonderful. One of these large canoes which the admiral measured was ninety-six feet long and eight feet broad. (Bernáldez, in Jane 1988, II:124)

THE BAHAMAS

Most modern visitors to the Bahamas, especially the smaller and drier islands, would not consider them preferable to northern Hispaniola or Cuba as a place to settle and practice subsistence agriculture and fishing. Today the islands at the southern end of the 1,000-km-long archipelago have a xeric vegetation and are badly eroded. The remaining soil is not very productive for farming, and the southern islands receive less than 800 mm of rainfall per year. Permanent streams are nonexistent and fresh groundwater is scarce. There is not a great deal of wild plant and animal food, at least on land (Keegan 1992:chapter 2).

Around A.D. 600, however, the situation was dramatically different. At that time the islands had lush tropical vegetation with substantial core areas of climax forest. Soils were rich and relatively deep, and fresh water was available on most islands. Wild plant and animal foods, including attractive foods such as monk seals and nesting sea turtles, would have been plentiful. There were also desirable resources, such as shells for bead making and good places for producing salt. The degradation of the Bahamian environment to its present state was the result of land-use practices of European colonists, who attempted to use the islands for intensive cultivation. In stripping the forests and clearing fields, they brought about massive erosion. They released pigs and goats on the islands, denuding the vegetation and out-competing the endemic fauna.

The story of the colonization of the Bahamas is similar to that of Jamaica in that it involved people responding to the regional situation and looking for new areas in which to settle. It was also similar in that people were moving into a new environment, well suited to their ways of growing food, as well as fishing and collecting wild sources of food. As with the Jamaican colonists, the Lucayans, as the people of the Bahamas were known, never lost touch with the people in the big islands to the south and continued to play a part in the Taíno world.

In his early interactions with the Lucayans, Columbus heard often of the islands to the south and the large ships and traders who were there. He also got a sense of the interactions within the islands, hearing of local rulers he called kings, who ruled several islands. Just a few days after his first landfall he noted,

> [A]fterward [I] returned to the ship and set sail, and I saw so many islands that I did not know how to decide which one I would go to first. And those men whom I had taken told me by signs that they were so very many that they were numberless. And they named by their names more than a hundred. Finally I looked for the largest and to that one I decided to go and so I am doing. It is about five leagues distant from this island of San Salvador, and the others of them some more, some less. All are very flat without mountains and very fertile and all populated and they make war on one another, even though these men are very simple and very handsome in body. (Sunday, 14 October 1492, Dunn and Kelley 1989:77)

The timing of the first colonization of the Bahamas is similar to that of Jamaica. The earliest sites date to around A.D. 600 to 700 and contain Ostionan pottery, similar to that found on Hispaniola and Jamaica (Carlson 1999; Keegan 1997b). Whether people first made the 90-km jump to the southern Bahamas from Hispaniola or Cuba is uncertain, as is the location of their earliest settlements. Keegan (1992:48–64) reviews the evidence and circumstances for several origins and points of landfall and leans toward Great Inagua or the Turks and Caicos. He notes that almost all of the sites on Great Inagua contain a lot of pottery that had been imported from the Greater Antilles, and there are possibly sites containing only imported pottery (Keegan 1992:62; see also Carlson 1999). One important early site is the Coralie Site (GT-3) on Grand Turk. This is one of the earliest sites in the Bahamas, and its pottery is all of an early Ostionoid style brought from the Greater Antilles (Carlson 1999). Based on the wood of a wild lime tree, its earliest date range is cal 650–790 A.D. (Carlson 1999:89). It is a substantial settlement with evidence of several house structures and multiple reoccupations, with access to rich resources such as green turtles and iguanas. The Coralie Site also shows another important aspect of the Bahamian paleoenvironment: the site today is barely above the water table and certainly would have been at a greater elevation above sea level at A.D. 700. The sea level has risen relative to the islands (or the islands have subsided), which further suggests that the southern islands in the Bahamian archipelago may have been larger, higher, wetter, and in richer in resources than at present (Carlson 1999; Keegan 1997b).

Another early site is located far up the Bahamian archipelago, nearly 400 km from Hispaniola, on the island of San Salvador (or Watling Island). There, Mary Jane Berman and Perry Gnivecki excavated the Three Dog Site in the late 1980s and 1990s (Berman and Gnivecki 1995). The site is located on the shores of a bay on the leeward, western side of the island. The site has an early component that Berman and Gnivecki (1991:174) date to A.D. 660–865, which is characterized by nonlocal Ostionan pottery. The pottery contains metamorphic inclusions that are not found in the Bahamas. They are thought to have been brought up through the islands from the south. The researchers find the best matches, in terms of the paste characteristics of the nonlocal pottery, at the sites of Arroyo del Palo, Mejias, and Madinga on the north coast of the eastern end of

Cuba (Berman and Gnivecki 1991:176). They propose a scenario in which the Bahamas were colonized over several centuries (roughly A.D. 600–900) by several groups, coming from various points of origin, including eastern Cuba and northern Hispaniola. The mixture of Ostionan and Meillacan pottery at Bahamian sites, as well as the locally made Palmetto pottery, reflects the complexity of a long process of colonization.

Another interesting thing the Three Dog Site demonstrates is that exploration and colonization in the Caribbean did not creep along gradually, island by island. The people who established a settlement at San Salvador may have passed many islands and cays to get there.

The work of William Keegan (1992), Betsy Carlson (1999), and others has been changing our understanding of the early human occupation of the Bahamas, bringing into focus the nature of early colonizing movements. Their work also shows the Bahamian sites not as small camps of explorers or people on the periphery of more populous areas but as important centers of craft specialization, resource extraction, trade, and political and ritual centralization.

CUBA

The situation in Cuba between A.D. 600 and 1000 involves a complex mix of migration from and interaction with people from Hispaniola. Also, the preceramic people who had been living on Cuba for nearly 5,000 years adopted some of the economic and cultural aspects of societies to the east. Telling the difference between transculturation and population movement in the archaeological record is difficult, but Cuban archaeologists have dealt with this issue very sensitively, creating a category of archaeological sites they call *la fase protoagricultores* (protoagricultural).

In the early 1960s archaeologists from the Academia de Ciencias de Cuba carried out research at the site of Arroyo del Palo, in the province of Mayarí in eastern Cuba. It is a small site, less than 50 m in length, running along an arroyo leading to the Río Mayarí. Archaeologist José Guarch visited the site in 1963 and realized that it contained some of the earliest known pottery from Cuba, with some stylistic connections to contemporary and earlier sites from

Hispaniola and Puerto Rico (Tabío and Guarch 1966). When Professors Tabío and Guarch carried out excavations there, they found that the Arroyo del Palo ceramics were included in archaeological deposits that otherwise would have been thought of as of the Cayo Redondo phase of the late preceramic. In other words, the lithics and other artifacts were consistent with the late preceramic, but there was also pottery that was reminiscent of, but not exactly like, that of the islands to the east. Interestingly, the site did not contain burenes or clay cassava griddles. This is significant because at all of the other Saladoid and Ostionoid sites, cassava griddles were an important part of the assemblage. Cassava was the staple domesticated plant that formed the basis of the subsistence system. Tabío and Guarch observed,

> Comparing the material from Arroyo del Palo with that which was studied by Rouse at the site of Ostiones, near Cabo Rojo on the western coast of Puerto Rico, which is the type site of the Ostionoid series (Rouse 1952), we can observe that the ceramics from the Cuban site present some few similarities with that from Ostiones in the following aspects: smooth finish, sides more or less upright or incurving, simple flat handles and simple red paint. Nevertheless, there exists the great difference consisting of the absence of cassava griddles [burenes] in Arroyo de Palo and the presence of these artifacts (sometimes decorated) in the Ostiones site. (Tabío and Guarch 1966:73)

They showed pictures of the Arroyo de Palo ceramics to Professor Rouse, who had worked in Cuba and Haiti as well as Puerto Rico, and he wrote back, "I agree with you that the ceramics of this site are equivalent to those of Meillac in Haiti, but I don't consider it to be the same style. My opinion is that there are sufficient differences to consider it a separate local development" (Tabío and Guarch 1966:72).

Since the excavation of Arroyo del Palo, many other protoagricultural sites have been found, as well as some whose ceramics have closer stylistic similarities to those on Hispaniola and Puerto Rico. In the Centro de Antropología's 1995 compact disk *Arqueología de Cuba* they list 67 protoagricultural sites of a sample of about 250 ceramics-bearing sites. So in Cuba, just as in Hispaniola, we must be careful about how we interpret the appearance of Ostionan-related ceramics, because what may seem to be a wave of migration may be to a large extent a pattern of shifting economic practices and technology adoption. I believe there is good evidence that both population movement and cultural change are involved during this period, and the interaction and synthesis of the preceramic people and the Saladoid descendants set the stage for the emergence of the Taíno polities.

GREATER ANTILLEAN CEREMONIALISM AND THE EMERGENCE OF TAÍNO POLITIES

Around A.D. 600 and before, there was little or any political organization that was above the village level. Villages were autonomous, and there was probably little internal differentiation in terms of social status. On the contrary, people had communal obligations to the group, and they probably had kinship ties to most of their neighbors as well.

By the time Columbus arrived in the Greater Antilles in 1492 there was a great deal of social differentiation and political elaboration. There were polities of more than 100 allied villages, with combined populations in the tens of thousands. There were well-defined and inherited social classes and at the top of the social and political hierarchy, high-ranking men and women who possessed a great deal of political power and social status. There were clear tiers in the social hierarchy, with caciques or chiefs coming from the elite group known as *nitaínos*. This term translates roughly as "us [the] good or noble" (Oliver 2005:8). Nitaínos probably comprised less than 5% of the population. Most of the Taíno people were in a commoner class, some possibly enslaved, who were called *naborías*, which means "the rest of them" (Oliver 2005:11).

So a remarkable change in sociopolitical organization had taken place in the centuries before contact, resulting in the rise of the complex Taíno polities known historically, and a good deal of recent research and scholarship has been directed at understanding this change (Chanlatte 1990; Curet 2003; Curet and Oliver 1998; Keegan, Maclachlan, and Byrne 1998; Siegel 2004; Veloz Maggiolo 1993; Wilson 1990, 2001).

In many respects these Caribbean societies encountered by the Europeans were comparable to middle-range societies or chiefdoms described in the Americas and elsewhere (Curet 2003; Drennan and Uribe 1987; Sahlins 1968). As many have observed, using labels such as *chiefdom* raises problems for many scholars, and some have concluded that it is more trouble than it's worth. For some the term seems either reductionistic, in that it may seem to assume that all societies thus named are in some way essentially the same, or naïve, because it seems to suggest logic of the form "Society X is a chiefdom; chiefdoms have these characteristics; therefore Society X must have these characteristics" (Curet 2003; Feinman and Neitzel 1984; Yoffee 2005, and others review these problems). The discussion that follows is primarily descriptive and particular to the Caribbean case rather than comparative and general about types of human political organization.

Part of the task of Caribbean archaeology has been to understand the emergence of the Taíno complex societies. What historical processes or events are related to this development? Where do we first find evidence for changes in social and political organization? Despite a great deal of discussion and debate among scholars, this has not been an area that has received targeted archaeological research in the Caribbean. To some extent this lack of direct research can be understood because of the ethnohistorical record for the Taíno – the eyewitness accounts by European observers of Taíno culture, society, and politics. This historical record was so good relative to the archaeological evidence for earlier periods that archaeologists turned their attention to less well known periods. They have explored a range of other topics: looking for the earliest evidence of human presence in the islands, tracking the early Saladoid movement up through the Lesser Antilles, conducting settlement survey, recording and interpreting rock art, understanding the adaptive strategies involving local and imported plants and animals, and many other research foci.

There are several archaeological sites that, together, shed new light on the processes involved in the emergence of the Taíno. They span the period in question and each site tells part of the story. It is a story, however, that is still poorly understood. The earliest is the Puerto Rican site of Maisabel, on the north coast of Puerto Rico. Next are the two best known sites with complexes of

ceremonial plazas (ball courts) in Puerto Rico – Tibes in the south
and Caguana in the west-central highlands. Finally, there are the sites
of El Atajadizo and Chacuey, in the Dominican Republic, on the
island of Hispaniola. This group of sites spans quite a long period
of time – over 1,000 years – but the developments that take place
at them, and the differences between them, help us to understand
the changes that took place as more complex forms of society were
invented in the Caribbean.

Maisabel is a large early ceramic site on the north coast of Puerto
Rico, about 30 km west of San Juan. It was excavated by Peter
Siegel, Peter Roe, and the Centro de Investigaciones Indígenas and
was the focus of Siegel's dissertation and several other publications
(Siegel 1989a, 1992). The Maisabel site covers about 20 ha and was
occupied from a century or two B.C. until around A.D. 1000 or
after. It is interesting in the context of the present discussion because
the site reflects the transition from a long Saladoid occupation to a
subsequent Ostionoid occupation and sheds light on what changes
might have taken place around A.D. 800–1000.

The site has a central open area, surrounded by areas of dense
midden refuse (Siegel 1992:figure 2.12). The middens are concentrated into five areas, but a general scatter of fairly dense ceramic
remains nearly surrounds the central area (Figure 4.4). Like many
Saladoid sites (and their South American relatives) the middens were
arrayed in a semicircle or circle around the central area. For the
Saladoid period (characterized by the local Hacienda Grande and
Cuevas styles of ceramics), the central area was used as a communal cemetery. This area was quite large – about 100 m across –
and Siegel excavated 23 burials there, primarily from the Saladoid
period. He estimates that there may be hundreds of burials in the
central cemetery (1989b:199). Siegel notes, "I do not think that it
is coincidental that the cemetery is at the precise center of the site.
This central portion of the site thus may be a visual, spatial, social,
and cosmological focal point for the early Ceramic age occupants of
Maisabel. I believe that this may accord with the ancestor cults associated with many of the South American lowland Indian groups . . ."
(Siegel 1989b:199). He relates several other features of the site, particularly large "mounded middens" that are adjacent to the central

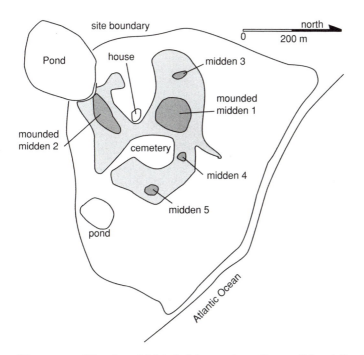

Figure 4.4. The site of Maisabel in northern Puerto Rico (after Siegel 1992:figure 2.12).

area, to a ceremonial program that is expressed in the site plan itself (1989b:204).

After the end of the Saladoid period, the use and nature of the central area seems to change. A few burials were found there, but it seems as if the preferred area for interment after A.D. 600 was in and around the houses, located in the ring of middens surrounding the central area. This is important because it may represent a shift away from burying one's family in the central communal space shared by the whole village and toward burying them in association with houses, which may have been spaces associated with discreet lineages or kinship groups. The central area does not get used for habitation or other use after A.D. 600 and may have been turned into a ceremonial plaza or ball court.

This story of Maisabel's central space is not completely clear, for there were a few burials that seem to postdate the Saladoid period

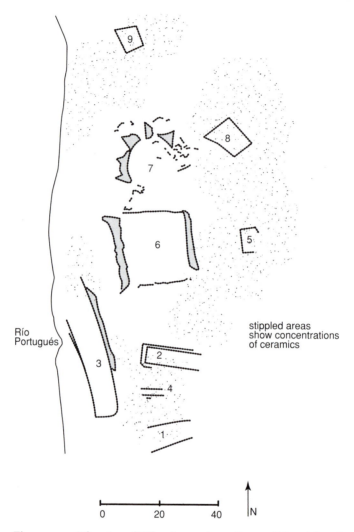

Figure 4.5. The site of Tibes in southern Puerto Rico (after Curet and Gracia 1995).

(or possibly they date to a transitional period) that were found in the central area. In general, however, Maisabel seems to reflect a shift from community to a lineage organization that is comparable to what seems to be happening at other contemporary sites (Curet and Oliver 1998).

Figure 4.6. Large circular plaza at Tibes, Puerto Rico.

One such site is Tibes, one of the most impressive complexes of ceremonial plazas in the Caribbean (Figure 4.5 and 4.6). It has 11 or more ceremonial plazas, most of them rectangular. It also has one circular feature, apparently with radiating triangles of cobble pavement (Curet and Rodríguez Garcia 1995; Curet and Oliver 1998; González Colón 1984). The site is about 8 km north of Puerto Rico's southern coast on the Río Portuguéz. It was first explored under the direction of González Colón, who also oversaw some reconstruction and stabilization of the site. It is now an archaeological park near the city of Ponce.

Beginning in the 1990s Antonio Curet, from the Field Museum of Natural History in Chicago, and an interdisciplinary team carried out extensive work at Tibes, working on all aspects of the site. Their aim was to understand the archaeological sequence associated with the emergence of one of the Caribbean's first complex societies. As was the case at Maisabel, Tibes contains both Saladoid and later Ostionoid components, but it was occupied longer and has a much more elaborated development of ball courts, ceremonial plazas, or stone-demarcated precincts (Figure 4.3). The largest of these plazas is located in the center of the site's architectural features. It is square and measures about 20 m on each side. The Tibes plazas probably date to around A.D. 700 to 900. Located beneath the central plaza was a Saladoid cemetery whose use predated the construction of the plaza (González Colón 1984). There was another cluster of Saladoid burials beneath Plaza 6 (Curet and Oliver 1998:225; González Colón 1984). Ostionoid burials were also found at Tibes, always in and around areas marked with later habitation debris. Once the stone-demarcated plazas were created, they were no longer used for burials.

In their article "Mortuary Practices in Precolumbian Puerto Rico" (1998), Antonio Curet and José Oliver use other ethnographic and historical cases to interpret the shift from centrally located, communal cemeteries to a dispersed pattern of burial in residential contexts. They argue that in Saladoid times, the kin-based descent group was the dominant unit of social organization ' the whole village (comprising group members and their in-marrying spouses), therefore people were buried in the central cemetery as an expression of this communal identity (Curet and Oliver 1998:228). That communal descent group was the basic organizing unit for both social and economic relations. Very little display of wealth or distinctiveness is ever seen in these early burials. Siegel (1989b, 1992) and Oliver (1993) also emphasized the importance of communal, kin-based villages during Saladoid time and traced the ethnographic and ethnohistoric links to South American groups, many of whom organized both their villages and their social relations in the same way (Heckenberger, Petersen, and Neves 1999).

In the later period, with the rise of greater social complexity, formal burial areas still reflect an individual's identity as part of a social unit, but that unit no longer was the dominant unit of social organization in the village. Individuals are buried with their own lineage or other social grouping or within the house of that group. What also increases between around A.D. 800 and the time of European contact is the expression of individual identity and status in the burial ritual. Within the competitive context of a Taíno polity, it became more important to demonstrate one's individual status to reinforce and enhance one's corporate status as a member of a competing lineage or kin-group. European observers recorded the practice of burying other individuals with a deceased cacique or leader, and stories of this practice, perhaps exaggerated, became part of the European narrative about the Taíno polities. Barlow's accounts of the early sixteenth-century voyage of Enciso (Barlow 1832) were the first extensive description of the Americas written in English, and he recorded this practice, as did many of his contemporaries:

> And when eny of the gret men of the indies which be called caciques die, thei make a gret hole in the ground wherin thei put him setting and sett before him both mete and drinke and so cover the hole ageine w^t tymbres and turves of earthe upon it, and leve open a hole as bigge as one maie scant go in at and then as many of his wyfes as do ernestlie love him take mete with them and goeth into the hole, and after thei be in thei cover the hole w^t tymbre and erthe so that thei can come no more owt ageyne, and thei have a belefe and saie thei go to acompany him to an other worlde when thei shal have more honor and pleasure then thei have here. (Barlow 1832:168)

The ceremonial center of Caguana is the most elaborate and complex center of its kind on Puerto Rico and represents a further development of Caribbean ceremonial centers (Figures 4.7 and 4.8). Caguana is located in west-central Puerto Rico, about 20 km from the north coast and 30 km from the south coast. In practical terms, it's a long way from either coast because it is in the rugged cock-pit country, characterized by steep hills, narrow valleys, and many caves and karst features. It is perched on a terrace on the side of a hill, looking down on a small river, and out across the conical mogote hills that surround the site.

Caguana shares many of the features of Tibes, and in fact, as can be seen in Figures 4.5 and 4.7, their spatial layouts are very comparable (Oliver 2005). Both sites are organized around a central plaza that is square and bounded by stones and aligned almost identically (probably to the stars or planets). Both have large circular features that articulate with the other features, and both have a series of smaller rectangular plazas or ball courts. There is also a chronological relationship between the two sites. Tibes had been a Saladoid village that developed into a ceremonial center between around A.D. 900. By around A.D. 1200, Tibes seems to have been in decline, but Caguana was experiencing a growth in size and importance (Oliver 2005:6–7). The ascendency of Caguana continued until the mid-1400s

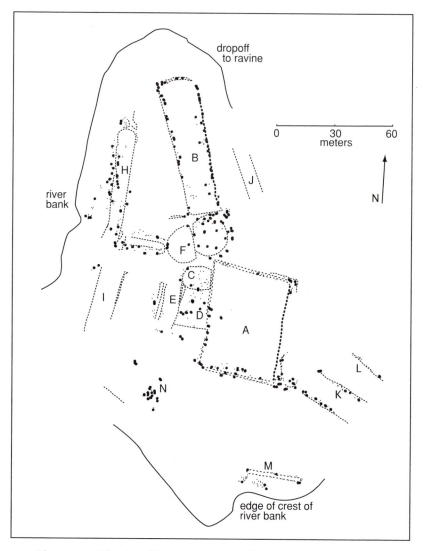

Figure 4.7. The site of Caguana in central Puerto Rico (after Mason 1941).

but apparently was in decline or had been abandoned by the time Europeans conquered the island of Puerto Rico in the early 1500s. There are no historical observations from the early contact period that can be firmly tied to Caguana.

Figure 4.8. Ceremonial plazas and cobbled pavements at Caguana, Puerto Rico.

As can be seen from the two plan maps (Figures 4.5 and 4.7), the sites of Tibes and Caguana (and many others) have large rectangular or square plazas, bounded by standing stones. At Caguana, many of the stones are as large as 2 m in height and some are carved with petroglyphs of anthropomorphic figures or faces or animals. The association of these stone-demarcated plazas at sites such as Tibes and Caguana with the ball game was made by the earliest European observers. The ball game itself was similar to that played in Mesoamerica and northern South America.

Two teams competed in trying to keep a solid rubber ball from bouncing more than once using any part of their bodies except their hands. They worked together to move the heavy ball toward one end of the court or the other. Las Casas (1967:537) describes the game as follows:

> Twenty or thirty stood at either end of the long enclosure. Those at one end would toss the ball to those at the opposite extreme and it was then smitten by whoever was nearest: with the shoulder, if the ball flew high, which the made the ball

return like lightning; and if it flew close to the ground, quickly putting their right hand to the ground and leaning on it, they would smite the ball with the point of a buttock which made the ball return more slowly. Those of the opposite side would likewise send it back with their buttock, until one or the other side committed a fault according to the rules of the game. It was a joyous sight to see when they played heated, especially when the women played with one another, they not hitting the ball with shoulder and buttock but with knees and I believe with their closed fists. (Alegría 1983:10)

The most important Taíno towns and ceremonial centers were organized around these plazas. Gonzalo Fernández de Oviedo y Valdez, in his *Historia General y Natural de las Indias* (1959, first published in 1525), notes that "in each [town] there was a place set aside in public squares and at the beginnings of their pathways for the ball game" (Alegría 1983:8). Bartolomé de Las Casas also comments on the place of the plazas in the Taíno villages:

> The towns in these islands were not arranged along their streets, save that the house of the king or lord of the town was built in the best place and upon the best site. In front of the royal residence there was a large clearing, better swept and smoother, more long than wide, which in the tongue of these islands they call batey, the penultimate syllable being long, which means the ball game. There were other houses too very near to this clearing, and if the town was a very large one there were other clearings or courts for the ball game which were of lesser size than the main one. (Alegría 1983:8)

The ball game was an important part of Taíno life. Some of the early chroniclers depict the game as community activity and entertainment. One can imagine the members of elite families sitting on ceremonial seats (*dujos*) around the stone-paved perimeter of the court and around them the population of several nearby villages. Betting on games is described, and in testimony collected by Jeronomite friars in 1517, Marcos de Aguilar described (or disparages) the people of Hispaniola and Puerto Rico as ". . . lazy, refusing to do aught save to hold *areytos* and play *batey*, a ball game, and to distill liquor with which they get drunk every night and to wash their bodies many times, both day and night, which is one of the things that shortens their lives for, coming out of an *areyto* or a game of *batey*, sweating, they jump into the water" (quoted in Alegria 1983:13). The observer's connection of activities in the plaza and water is significant, because many of the plazas are connected to nearby streams or pools with a causeway or stone-lined path, extending the special character of the plaza space to a place of bathing. Typically the bathing area would have many petroglyphs and paintings around it.

In addition to being the focus of communal activity, the ball game was an important way that different polities (*cacicazgos*) interacted. Some ball courts are found in areas between polities and may have been a place where a whole range of interactions could have taken place, including ceremonies, trade, intermarriage, and other exchanges. There is, for example, evidence of three ball courts on the little island of Mona (about 8 km in diameter), midway between eastern Hispaniola and western Puerto Rico. Mona would have been a difficult place for large numbers of people to live but a good place for interisland meetings (Alegría 1983:113–14).

In the foregoing quotes, mention was made of *areytos*, which involve dance, song, and sometimes oral performance. The *areytos* include a range of ceremonial performances at the center of the Taíno spiritual world and one of the main ways that living people interacted with spirit beings. In his *Historia de las Indias*, Las Casas describes one *areyto* as follows:

> ... out came infinite people and many señores and nobility, whose seats were of all the province of the king Behecchio and the queen, his sister, Anacaona, singing their songs and dancing their dances, which they called *areytos*, things that were very pleasant and agreeable to see, especially when their numbers were great; out came 30 women, who were kept as wives of the king Behecchio, all completely naked, only covering their private parts with half-skirts of cotton, white and very elaborate in their style of weaving, which they call naguas, which cover from the belt to the middle of the leg; they were carrying green branches in their hands, singing and dancing and jumping with moderation, as is suitable for women, and showing great peace, delight, happiness and the spirit of a party. They all arrived in front of Don Bartolomé Colón, and they went down on their

knees on the earth, with great reverence, and gave him the branches and palms which they carried in their hands. . . . (Las Casas, 1951 I:441)

José Oliver's analysis of the ceremonial plazas centers on the *areytos*. He notes, "The areíto (or areyto) was without a doubt the principal ceremony enacted in the large central, quadrangular plaza of civic-ceremonial centers, such as Tibes and Caguana" (Oliver 2005:24). He describes the drumming, chanting, and taking of hallucinogenic substances involved in the interaction of elites and the spiritual world, and in his analysis the many petroglyphs that adorn the standing slabs of stone play an important role:

> It is this central, quadrangular plaza in Caguana where the ensemble – a community – of 40 plus petroglyph icons articulated in ceremonial ritual with humans. These, rather than the buried community of deceased ancestors of the ancient Saladoids, are the ones who comprised the 'community' of numinous being engaged in areítos. But while the 'message' for the Saladoid was to reinforce their corporate, kin-based values, in Caguana the 'message' is to reinforce the centrality of the institution of cacique as the means to maintain solidarity. (Oliver 2005:25)

Areytos were performed at a variety of occasions, including deaths, births, marriages, declarations of war or peace, and the arrival or departure of important visitors, and many times they weren't particularly solemn or reverent. Oviedo describes the participants and dancers' use of some kind of alcoholic drink, drinking without stopping the *areyto*, with the ceremony ending when all of the participants passed out (see Oliver 2005:29). We should be careful to avoid drawing the conclusion that these ceremonies were drunken parties, as some early observers clearly believed. Rather, the purpose of the *areyto* was to connect the world of the living with the spirit world in a way that was relevant to the living, and this often involved attaining altered states of consciousness (Arrom 1975; Oliver 2005; Roe 2005).

One of the characteristics of Caguana and Tibes (but not most of the large single-plaza centers of Hispaniola still to be discussed) is that apart from the large central plaza, there are many other smaller ones. Oliver (2005) and others (Siegel 1992; Curet and Oliver 1998) suggest that the large, central plazas are associated with reinforcing the shared identity of the entire community and would have been used for events involving everyone. Oliver sees the smaller, rectangular courts, often lined with stones only on the two long sides, as being used by subgroups – lineages, perhaps, or residents of a particular part of the territory served by the ceremonial center. The smaller plazas are probably more closely associated with the ball game itself rather than with *areytos* (Oliver 2005:26–7). The site of Caguana was a meeting place, probably for people that were fairly widely dispersed in smaller communities. It was not itself a large habitation site. So the many smaller plazas may somehow reflect the diversity of people who came, either geographically or in terms of kinship groups or other crosscutting associations.

CEREMONIAL CENTERS OF HISPANIOLA

On the island of Hispaniola Taíno ceremonial sites are arranged differently. There are fewer ball courts on Hispaniola than on Puerto Rico (21 and 65 known, respectively). Also, many of the Hispaniola sites only have one plaza, often a very large one. These differences may reflect the cultural differences between Puerto Rico and Hispaniola. On Puerto Rico the Saladoid ancestry of the people who lived there was very pronounced, even with the history of cultural interaction and synthesis with the preceramic or Archaic people that had taken place on Puerto Rico as much as 1,000 years previously. On Hispaniola, as we have seen, the cultural interaction between Puerto Rican Ostionoid people and the Archaic inhabitants of the island was still in effect going on. There was still a great deal of cultural diversity on the island, which would last into the contact period and which is reflected in the regional variants of late ceramic pottery across the island. Just as the people of Hispaniola transformed the older ways of decorating pottery when they adopted that technology, we may expect that they transformed the social and political institutions associated with the ball game, *areytos*, and Taíno ceremonialism generally. Before considering the nature of all these differences, it is necessary to look at some of the Hispaniola sites in detail.

EL ATAJADIZO

The site of El Atajadizo is near the southeastern coast of the Dominican Republic, at the mouth of the Yuma River. This *Boca de Yuma* region has been the focus of considerable research by the Museo del Hombre Dominicano (Veloz Maggiolo, Ortega, and Sanoja 1976a). El Atajadizo began as a late Ostionoid site and developed into a Chicoid center with a central plaza and other architectural features. It seems to represent the continuity of Puerto Rican ideas about ceremonial plazas but with some differences and developments, especially in the use of cobbled pavements and causeways.

The nearby preceramic component of the area is called Musié Pedro and probably dates to the last few centuries B.C. and after (Veloz Maggiolo, Vargas, Sanoja, and Luna Calderon 1976b:288, report an uncorrected radiocarbon date of 2255 ± 80 or 305 B.C., I-8646). It is located about 1 mile north of the main plaza at El Atajadizo. It contains flint tools comparable to other Archaic occupations on the island, as well as ground stone tools, conch picks, and coral tools.

The beginning of the ceramic period occupation at El Atajadizo is much later, probably around A.D. 800. Veloz Maggiolo and his colleagues have one radiocarbon date of A.D. 840 ± 80 for this phase (I-8649, Veloz Maggiolo *et al.* 1976b:287). The pottery from this period, which is called the Atajadizo phase, is characterized by polished surface treatments on red and cream vessels, comparable to other Ostionoid settlements. There is some modeling, incision, and applied modeled or incised decorations, as well as the use of punctation, sometimes in zones.

The spatial organization of the Atajadizo phase village is not clear because it was built over in later times but is located in the same general area as the habitation area surrounding the later plaza. The Ostionoid village and its houses and features may have been arrayed around the open area that later was made into the plaza. Burials in the Atajadizo phase were located next to the interior walls of houses.

These houses were built at the natural ground level of the site. In later times, mounded middens had been built up and were used as raised foundations for houses and, later, for use as burial mounds (Luna Calderon 1976; Veloz Maggiolo *et al.* 1976a, 1976b).

The Guayabal phase, probably dating from after A.D. 1000 to 1300 or so, is characterized by more specialized use of space at the site. The central plaza is built at this time. Veloz Maggiolo and colleagues (1976b) report its total surface area as 1456.1 sq m (about 30 × 50 m). It has a cobbled pavement on the northwest end and is surrounded by stones set vertically. The researchers located remnants of a cobbled pavement extending from this plaza toward the nearby Duey River. This feature may have extended more than 100 m. There is another feature about 150 m from the main plaza that the excavators call Plaza B. The part of it that remains is about 40 × 15 m. It is another pavement of cobbles, apparently with a circular area in the middle without stones. There was probably more to this feature, and indeed other cobbled pavements had been present at the site, but they have been destroyed by modern agricultural activity. Around the plaza and especially to the south and east of it are five mounds, ranging from about 20–40 m wide and about 1 to 2 m high. Some of these are interpreted as midden mounds that were used as burial mounds in the last phase of the site's use. There are other areas of habitation that are some distance from the central plaza that do not exhibit this kind of mounded construction, leading the authors to conclude the mounds were intentionally constructed as house platforms or cemeteries (Veloz Maggiolo *et al.* 1976b:283–8).

The site of El Atajadizo clearly shares some characteristics with sites such as Tibes and Caguana on Puerto Rico. The central plaza is similar to, but is slightly smaller than, the main plaza at Caguana (1456.1 sq m at Atajadizo vs. 1761 sq m at Caguana). Its orientation is different – more southeast to northwest instead of roughly north–south as at Caguana and Tibes. The Atajadizo plaza is bounded by standing stones, however, and portions of the perimeter have areas of cobbled pavements. There was apparently a greater importance attached to causeways or cobbled sidewalks in the Dominican Republic site, and this may be an indication of a change that will become more elaborated in later sites. El Atajadizo has the large

cobbled pavement feature, the Plaza B mentioned above, with a
causeway leading from it to the northeast part of the site. Finally
there is the cobbled causeway going from the plaza to the river, a
feature that can be seen at several other later sites on Hispaniola. In
a way these features take on equal or greater significance, extending
the special nature of the ball court or ceremonial plaza and connecting it to a river and to other features of the site. Another difference
is that El Atajadizo doesn't have the multiple rectangular ball courts
of Caguana and Tibes. On Hispaniola the special nature of the ceremonial plaza is retained, but the focus seems to be more on *areytos*
as key displays of chiefly power and less on the ball game itself.

THE ZONE OF CHACUEY

In the northwest part of the Dominican Republic, near the Río
Chacuey and about 20 km from the north coast, there is a Taíno
ceremonial center that differes in scale and organization from those
in Puerto Rico and Boca de Yuma that we have discussed. In many
ways it continues some of the traditions of the earlier plazas: it uses
stone causeways or pavements to mark off a ceremonial space; there
are standing stones with petroglyphs associated with the plaza; there
is a surrounding pavement or causeway and attached areas of wider
pavements that provide a viewing area for people to watch what
takes place within; the plaza is connected to a river by two parallel
causeways; and at the river, there is a bathing pool with many petroglyphs around it, which reproduce some of the anthropomorphic
figures, faces, and other characters found at Caguana. The site was
investigated in the early 1950s by Emile Boyrie de Moya, Director
of the Instituto Dominicano de Investigaciones Anthropológicas at
the Universidad de Santo Domingo (Boyrie de Moya 1955).

What is different about the site at Chacuey is its scale. The area
enclosed in the ceremonial plaza is 250 m on its longest axis, which is
aligned roughly northeast to southwest (Figure 4.9). It is about 145 m
wide, and the interior surface area is 29,000 sq m. The combined
surface area of all of the plazas at Caguana is less than 5,500 sq m.
The perimeter of the Chacuey plaza is 659 m, and the stone paved
causeway that surrounds it varies between 4.5 and 5 m in breadth;

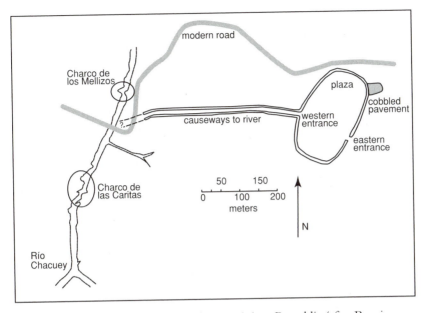

Figure 4.9. The site of Chacuey in the Dominican Republic (after Boyrie de Moya 1955).

it is between 40 and 80 cm high. There is also a stone pavement in the northeast corner that is 40 × 25 m. The double causeway leading to the Río Chacuey has not completely survived but would have been over 600 m in length (Boyrie de Moya 1955:43–9). The parallel causeways are each between 3 and 3.5 m in width and are made of the same stone cobbles covered with soil as the perimeter of the plaza. These are between 25 and 70 cm in height, depending on deposition conditions along the slope (the plaza is on a plateau 51 m above the river). The distance between the two causeways, from center to center, is 13.60 m, leaving an interior surface at least 10 m in breadth. Where the two causeways enter the plaza there were two *menhires* or monoliths guarding the entrance, as Boyrie de Moya (1955:49) describes them. They are less than 1 m high and were engraved with simple anthropomorphic faces comparable to those at Caguana.

The size of the plaza perimeter and the extent and size of the causeways leading from it attest to the amount of effort that went into its construction. The paved surface or *calzada* around the plaza has a volume of mounded earth and stone of about 1,700 cu m. The parallel causeways leading to the river also represent about 1,700 cu m of cobble and earth construction, and the cobbled pavement beside the plaza is another 600 cu m. The total of about 4,000 cu m is impressive and an indication of the importance of the plaza to the *caciques*, their lineages, and the community. This volume does not approach the size of other well-known monuments from other areas of the Americas; Temple I at Tikal has a volume of about 15,000 cu m, and other large pyramid structures at Teotihuacan, Cholula, or Cahokia are much larger.

The area near the Chacuey River was covered with petroglyphs, many of which have survived. Two areas are heavily inscribed, and Boyrie de Moya called them the "Pool of the Twins" (*Chaco de las Mellizos*) and the "Pool of the Little Faces" (*Chaco de las Caritas*). Together these places provide an area of perhaps more than 100 separate carvings, some simple faces, some complex scenes with more than one person or animal. The interpretation of this important body of figurative information, so clearly tied to the Caribbean peoples' myth and history as recorded by Pané (1974) and other chroniclers, has developed very impressively in recent years (Arróm 1997; Oliver 1998, 2005; Roe 1993, 2005). The ideographic material at Chacuey deserves to be considered in the same way, probably representing Taíno practices shortly before European conquest.

Describing the ceramics from the site, Marcio Veloz Maggiolo notes, "the ceramic material associated with the causeway of the Corral de los Indios de Chacuey can be classified as an extension of the Boca Chica style, similar in some aspects to the nearby ceramics expressed at the site of Carrier, in Haiti [which is about 40 km to the northwest]" (1972:169–70). The pottery from Chacuey is not extensively described in Boyrie's 1955 report, but it seems clear from the illustrations that as Veloz Maggiolo suggests, the ceramics from the site are comparable to other late sites on Hispaniola.

According to an article in the Boletín of the Museo del Hombre Dominicano, the plaza at Chacuey was badly damaged by road construction in 1980–1982 (Marichal 1989:95–100). It is not clear how extensive the damage is, but this is a site of enormous importance to

the cultural patrimony of the Dominican Republic and the Caribbean. Unfortunately, nearly all archaeological sites in the Caribbean
region are both threatened to some extent and inadequately pro-
tected by law.

The scale of the site at Chacuey is impressive, but it's not a unique
instance or even the largest site of its kind on Hispaniola. A comparable site is to be found about 80 km south at the site of Corral de
los Indios at San Juan de la Maguana. It is on the other side of the
Cordillera Central, therefore it would have been a longer journey
on foot. The Corral de los Indios is an oval plaza, surrounded by
a single, wide, raised platform, like the perimeter of the Chacuey
site. In 1851 it was described by Sir Robert Schomburgk as being a
raised cobblestone pavement 21 feet in width, with a total circum-
ference of 2,270 feet or 691 m. The area encompassed in the plaza is
much larger than any other known plaza in the Caribbean – about
43,000 sq m. Veloz Maggiolo suggests that an unfortunate attempt
at restoration in 1925 changed the configuration of the site, divid-
ing the single external ring described by Schomburgk into two. I
believe, from a visit to the site in the 1980s, that there may have been
remnants of one or more causeways leading from the plaza toward
the nearby stream. There is a large stone in the center of the plaza
that was described by both Schomburgk (1851) and Boyrie de Moya
(1955:54–61). It is about 1.5 m in height and has a simple petroglyph
of a face with an open oval mouth on it. It is known locally as the
"stone of Anacaona" (Peguero Guzman 2001:55).

The Corral de los Indios at San Juan de la Maguana is one of
the few archaeological sites that can confidently be associated with
the early historical account written by Europeans. It was the seat of
one of Hispaniola's most powerful *caciques*, Caonabo. His principal wife was Anacaona, a very high-ranking member of the ruling
lineage of a neighboring polity (*cacicazgo*) that was centered on the
plain where modern Port-au-Prince sits. According to Las Casas
(1951 I:406–7) the village around Corral de los Indios was where the
cacique Caonabo was captured by the Spanish. The story (discussed at
more length in an earlier work, Wilson 1990:84–9) involves a visit
by Alonzo de Hojeda to this place in 1494 to attempt to capture
the indigenous ruler, who was considered to be the greatest threat

to the few Europeans who were then on the island. In a story that seems to have been embellished, de Hojeda is said to have tricked Caonabo by giving him a highly polished set of shackles, saying they came from the sky. Caonabo felt secure, in the middle of his own province, surrounded by thousands of his own people. Alonzo de Hojeda allowed Caonabo to ride on his horse in front of him and then snapped the shackles shut and took off with his captive, leaving the village at Corral de los Indios behind them.

A few other very large ceremonial plazas are located on Hispaniola, showing a change from many small plazas in a complex to a single large one and usually with causeways connecting the plaza to water. One such site is Plaza La Cacique, near the town of Monción in the north-central part of the island. It was also investigated by Boyrie de Moya (1960). Quoting Veloz Maggiolo's description,

> Its characteristics are very similar to the ceremonial plazas of San Juan de la Maguana and Chacuey. . . . The plaza is elliptical, with a length of 132 m on its major axis and 77 m length on the minor axis. It is surrounded by tall embankments of earth 1.5 meters in height, with a base seven to eight meters in breadth. The parallel causeways going away from the plaza are separated by nine meters, and are 250 meters long. They go to the west until the reach a stream that drains towards the Arroyo Naranjo and in this stream along one of its banks, there is, as in the case of Chacuey, an interesting complex of petroglyphs. (Veloz Maggiolo 1972:167)

CUBA

Cuba has only a few of the ceremonial plazas, but they are very large, comparable to those in Hispaniola, and clustered in the eastern tip of the island. At the site of Pueblo Viejo, in the easternmost province of Guantanamo, there is a village with a large rectangular enclosure that is about 250 m long on its longest axis. It sits on a mesa overlooking the Windward Passage between Haiti and Cuba. It was first described by the Spanish geographer Miguel Rodríguez Ferrer in the mid-1800s, who drew connections between these earthworks and those of the Mississippian Period in North America and the large temples and other constructions of Mesoamerica (Alegría 1983:17–21). As had happened in North America, when early observers of the large earthworks refused to believe that they had been created by Native Americans, Rodríguez Ferrer declined to believe that these large plazas were the work of the people who met Columbus. He said,

> All of these relics, all these memorials, are tangible traces, assured evidence, of the passing through Cuba of a people who left all these vestiges. I can assign no date to this race and people, but rest assured that these were not of the same race and people as the natives that Columbus found in Cuba. (quoted in Alegría 1983:17)

The site Rodríguez Ferrer mentions, Pueblo Viejo, has a large enclosure made of mounded gravel and cobbles. Stewart Culin, visiting around the turn of the twentieth century from the University of Pennsylvania, described it as follows:

> The embankment, some twelve or fifteen feet wide at the base and 10 feet in height, was 668 feet long. . . . I found that it formed a rectangular enclosure, with sides extending back to another ridge some 300 feet, its greatest length being in a line east and west. It was manifestly the work of human hands, the gravel having been brought from a distance. The interior of the square, which was planted with bananas, was bare of trees. Its soil was dark in color, quite unlike the reddish clay of the surrounding country, and mixed with fragments of coars, reddish-black pottery. (quoted in Alegría 1983:18)

José M. Guarch described the site in his 1972 monograph, *Excavaciones en el extremo oriental de Cuba*, and illustrates modeled and incised pottery comparable to Taíno sites on Hispaniola.

Clearly, the plaza at Pueblo Viejo is comparable to the largest ceremonial constructions in the Caribbean. It encloses approximately 23,000 cu m and its perimeter wall is about 680 m long. Like so many monumental sites discussed in this chapter, Pueblo Viejo has been significantly damaged in recent decades, but it would be very interesting to carry out additional work there to determine how the plaza connects to habitation areas and nearby water, and how it relates to comparable sites on the eastern tip of Cuba.

The nearby site of Laguna Limones, also near the coast, also has a large rectangular earthwork, this one about 153 × 80 m. It is described by several authors as having an opening on the southeastern corner, and to the south of the opening are nine midden mounds, giving evidence of a sizable population at the site (Guarch 1972:29–32; Tabío and Rey 1966:199–205). There is also, as the site's name suggests, a lagoon or natural pond about 100 m from the opening of the enclosure.

There is at least one other site on the eastern end of Cuba with these large earthen features, and several others, as Alegría describes, that possibly have them and deserve additional study. In his two-volume work called *Cuba Before Columbus* (1921), Mark Harrington describes the earthwork at Monte Cristo as follows: "Revisiting the site in 1919 we found that the embankment formed the eastern end of what had been a parallelogram with rounded corners, about 150 feet across, the embankment being fully five feet high at its highest point; but when we tried to trace it westward, where it extended in to the brush, we soon lost it amid the tangle, for here the walls were much lower" (Harrington 1921, 2:38). He also describes two well-defined mounds, one apparently within the enclosure and one outside.

A final site that appeared to have large earthen walls is near the Maya River, also near Punta Maisí, on the eastern tip of the island. Harrington (1921, 2:279) called it the "Big Wall Site." He interpreted a long and deep midden on the eastern part of the site as part of an earthen enclosure, but Guarch's later excavations (1972) suggest instead that the wall was a linear midden mounded up on a natural rise. The site does suggest intensive occupation over a long period, which is important given the presence of the three large earthen enclosures that are nearby.

Cuba's plazas show that the indigenous people of this part of Cuba were very much involved in the kind of Taíno ceremonialism that we see on Hispaniola and Puerto Rico, as well as in the Bahamas and probably Jamaica. It is interesting to note that the plazas in Cuba are all of the single, large sort, most comparable to those of the western Dominican Republic (e.g., Plaza La Cacique, Chacuey, or San Juan de la Maguana). What is particularly notable is that the plazas on Cuba, and some others that may be plazas, are all clustered together at the eastern tip of the island, all within about 20 km of each other or less. An interesting question for the future is whether this area represents a beachhead for the expansion of a *cacicazgo* from Hispaniola into eastern Cuba, the local development of a distinctive Cuban style of Taíno ceremonialism, or some combination of those two interpretations.

SUMMARY POINTS CONCERNING CEREMONIAL PLAZAS

The very large ceremonial plazas of Hispaniola seem to represent another change in the sequence of developments that led from Saladoid times to the historically known Taíno polities. In Puerto Rico, we saw some earlier shifts in site organization relating to social organization. Initially, sites such as Maisabel were organized around a central clearing that served as a communal cemetery. As Curet and Oliver (1998) and Siegel (2004) have argued, this suggests a pattern of social, political, and economic organization that is organized around extended social groupings, most likely kin-groups of some sort. As Curet and Oliver note, "[t]his ideology and custom probably originated in, and subsequently diverged from, the traditions brought to the Antilles from South America by the early Saladoid immigrants" (1998:233).

In post-Saladoid times the emphasis of corporate display shifts from emphasizing the individual's connection to the community to elaborating the connection to his or her lineage. Burials, with the accumulated achievement and honor of the deceased, are now in houses, and the communal cemetery becomes a locus of ceremony. There was likely growing competition between lineages, which were increasingly ranked in terms of their relative status. This may have been expressed as competition between villages, to some degree ritualized in the ball game and surrounding festivities. Like a lot of Greater Antillean interactions from this time forward, "peer-polity interaction" seems to be a good way of referring to the relations among autonomous polities as they imitated each other, competed, traded, intermarried, combined, diverged, and underwent sociopolitical change (Renfrew and Cherry 1986). The ball game, played in ceremonial plazas at places such as Tibes and Caguana (and 60 or more related centers around Puerto Rico), was an important focus for this interaction. The auxiliary courts and plazas may have been associated with individual lineages or groups, but the central plaza still represented the overall coherence of the polity.

Taíno social and political organization changed again after the time when these large, multiplaza sites were the most important centers in the Caribbean. What happened was that the competition between lineages became a struggle to demonstrate a lineage's, and even an individual chief's, superior ancestry and connection to supernatural beings. The way in which this pedigree and connection to powerful *cemís* was manifested was through *areytos*, performed in the sacred context of the ceremonial plaza. As the glorification of the *cacique* and his lineage became more and more important, the primary function of the plaza changed from being the site of the ball game to being the stage for the *areyto*. We can see the performance of lineage status often in the early chronicles, for example, in the way the *cacique* of Xaraguá was referred to in this passage from Martyr,

> Beuchios Anacauchoa was also called Tareigua Hobin, which means "prince resplendent as copper." So likewise Starei, which means "shining"; Huibo, meaning "haughtiness"; Duy-heiniquem, meaning a "rich river." Whenever Beuchios Ana-cauchoa publishes an order, or makes his wishes known by her-alds' proclamation, he takes great care to have all these names and forty more recited. If, through carelessness or neglect, a single one were omitted, the cacique would feel himself grievously outraged; and his colleagues share this view. (Martyr 1970: I:387)

It is possible to view the very large ceremonial plazas of Hispaniola, located at the centers of these large polities, as monuments to the status of the *cacique* and indeed the *cacicazgo*. As Oliver argues, *areytos* "are ceremonies whose entire action and motion speaks of structure, maximum order, unity of purpose and, significantly, submission to leadership" (2002:29). He quotes Las Casas's description of an *areyto* in which 300 to 400 people danced impressively in lock-step, "in such a way that not even one foot would be out of step more than the tip of a needle" (Las Casas 1967, vol. I). What a powerful *cacique* needed, then, was a heroic lineage, powerful *cemís*, a large plaza, and a lot of followers. What we see in both the archaeology and ethnohistory of the Taíno is the desire and efforts of powerful lineages to line up all of these important elements.

The foregoing is a model of what was happening in the Caribbean shortly before European conquest. Taking a more general survey of the situation in the Greater Antilles, we see a diversity of polities, strategies, and archaeological manifestations in terms of plazas. In Puerto Rico there are many *caciques* and many plazas and plaza complexes. It is difficult to identify "paramount" chiefs with broad influence or authority across the island. They may have existed and their authority had fallen apart before the situation was recorded by early European observers, but there is not a readily apparent "paramount site" whose size and scale reflects a paramount chief. Rather, there were probably many local *caciques* and perhaps to some degree a "first among equals" depending on the circumstances. The plazas in Puerto Rico tend to be rectangular and bounded with standing stones.

Hispaniola was divided into five or so large *cacicazgos* (Charlevoix 1731:1733; Vega 1980; Wilson 1990) and had a number of large plazas, at least one of which we know corresponded to one of the most powerful chiefs. The archaeological presence of a large plaza does not necessarily mean that there was a paramount chief there, for a *cacicazgo's* power resided in the chiefly person, heroic lineage, powerful *cemís*, large following, and so on. The large plaza was a stage setting that was incomplete without the rest. What we may be seeing in easternmost Cuba, where several large plazas crowd a small area, is a record of competition between competing individuals or groups, each vying for power and a following. Even if one center did gain dominance over the others, however, it might be for only a time.

On Hispaniola there are large plazas surrounded with wide cobbled pavements in the west-central part of the island and smaller rectangular plazas with standing stones like at El Atajadizo in the southeast. There are several others that are made simply of parallel earthen embankments (Alegría 1983). In eastern Cuba there are large earthen rectangles, often with evidence of habitation on the tops of the walls. On Jamaica, despite ethnohistoric evidence for the kinds of ceremonies described above, no plazas have yet been found. At least one plaza center is known from the southern Bahamas.

This range of diversity in the architecture of plazas derives from three factors: chronology, function, and cultural variability. Chronology simply acknowledges that plazas evolved through many configurations between about A.D. 700 and 1500 and that many relict forms have probably been found. Functional differences reflect the plazas changing use from ball game court to central performance space, as the nature of political organization changed. Architectural differences that reflect cultural diversity and are regionally clustered seem to exist, but they are difficult to disentangle from the other two factors based on physical evidence alone. In Chapter 5 the cultural diversity of Caribbean on the eve of European contact will be explored.

THE CARIBBEAN ON THE EVE
OF EUROPEAN CONTACT

In the last few centuries before the arrival of Columbus and others from Europe, the people of the Caribbean were in the midst of change throughout the archipelago. From the smallest islands, where local groups struggled to make the most of the available resources and relationships with other groups, to the largest polities, which confronted large-scale and powerful forces of change, the people of the Caribbean were undergoing profound transformations.

This final chapter explores the cultural and political situation in late prehistory, paying attention to processes and directions of change, particularly to the following categories and engines of ongoing transformation:

- The processes of cultural change involved in the growth in complexity of the Taíno polities were still very important. Large-scale changes were taking place on Hispaniola and Puerto Rico, but there was also a significant impact on Cuba, Jamaica, and the Bahamas. *Cacicazgos* were emerging in places they had not been previously, and the attendant competition among lineages and individuals for status and power was itself a powerful force for change (Keegan *et al.* 1998; Wilson 1990).
- A related force, which was changing the political geography of the Caribbean, was the continuing growth of the largest polities. These large *cacicazgos*, especially on Hispaniola, were

attaining new levels of size and territorial expansion. The polities of the Greater Antilles were beginning to project their influence into the Lesser Antilles and certainly into neighboring parts of the Greater Antilles and the Bahamas (Hofman 1993; Keegan 1992).

- The processes of cultural differentiation and regional adaptation were continuing. Despite the relative interconnectedness of the Caribbean, where canoe travel easily linked the islands, some groups remained isolated. Over the generations and centuries, the various regions were developing in distinctive directions in terms of language, cultural practice, settlement patterns, economy, extent of long-distance interaction, and relationship to the environment (Wilson 1993).

- At the same time, in some parts of the region a more significant factor was the ongoing process of cultural interaction, conflict, and synthesis and the degree of cultural hybridity that emerged from these forms of culture contact (Kapchan and Strong 1999). So many parts of the Caribbean were populated by people with multiple ancestries – for example, the centuries-long interaction of Archaic people with the more recently arrived Saladoid people from South America – that cultural diversity was undoubtedly an important part of prehistoric Caribbean life (Chanlatte 1990).

- Finally, the people of the Caribbean were in ongoing contact with people from the surrounding mainlands. In the Lesser Antilles this interaction had been important almost as long as people had lived there, and it seemed to have grown in importance just before and after European contact. In the Greater Antilles this interaction is more difficult to see archaeologically, but there is historic evidence for contact with Central and South America.

All of these processes and forces were in play in the Caribbean, often with many of them having an influence at the same. The following discussion attempts to track their impact while considering the general state of affairs in the last few centuries before contact.

CULTURAL DIVERSITY IN THE GREATER ANTILLES

In later prehistory, it is possible to see similarities in ceramic decoration over a wide area in the Greater Antilles and northwestern Lesser Antilles. Potters used deep incision and elaborate sculptural modeling to embellish mostly unpainted vessels and effigies. The patterns of parallel lines and punctations, as well as repetitive scrolling lines and chevrons, are echoed in other media. Woodcarving was a fine art in the Greater Antilles, and we are lucky that many extraordinary objects have survived. Sculptures in bone and also woven into cotton evoke a powerful and distinctive style that we associate with the Taíno, including everything from St. Croix on the east to Cuba on the west and from Jamaica up into the Bahamas (see Kerchache 1994 or Bercht, Farmer, and Taylor 1997 for examples). Archaeologists identify it most clearly with the ceramics from the Boca Chica region of the southeast coast of the Dominican Republic, and Rouse has used the term *Chican Ostionoid* to refer to this suite of decorative modes and vessel shapes.

It is tempting, given the extensive archaeological distribution of these traits, to see a Chican "horizon" spreading from Cuba back into the northern Lesser Antilles and imagine that it represents some degree of cultural homogeneity across that distance. Other archaeological evidence, however, challenges this view. One of the most profound sets of differences separates the archaeology of Puerto Rico and Hispaniola. In her 1997 dissertation, "Ideographic Expression in the Precolumbian Caribbean," Shirley McGinnis explored a database of over 1,000 symbolic artifacts from the Caribbean, looking for patterns and differences from place to place. Comparing late artifacts on these two islands she made the following observations:

- In Hispaniola far greater emphasis was placed on the paraphernalia of the cohoba ritual (in which a psychoactive snuff was used to induce ritual hallucination) than in Puerto Rico. McGinnis (1997) had records of 16 "drug tables" in Hispaniola but none from Puerto Rico (Figure 5.1). In the Jeronomite friar Ramón Pané's unique record of Taíno religion made in the

Figure 5.1. Human effigy drug table of carved wood from the Dominican Republic, 67 cm tall (after Kerchache 1994:114).

mid-1590s (Arrom 1975; Bourne 1906; Stevens-Arroyo 1988) he describes their use: "each [cacique has] . . . a house apart from the village . . . in which they have a finely wrought table, round like a wooden dish in which some powder rests, which is placed by them on the heads of these cemís in performing a certain ceremony; then with a cane that has two branches which they place in the nostrils they snuff up this dust. . . . With this powder they lose consciousness and become like drunken men" (Bourne 1906:311–12). There is also a form of pestle associated with grinding the powder used in this ritual and McGinnis counts 33 of them from Puerto Rico and 238 from Hispaniola.

Figure 5.2. Detail from the end of a manatee-rib vomiting spatula from the Dominican Republic, 26.3 cm long, Fundación García Arévalo (after Kerchache 1994:81).

Another part of this ritual was purifaction through vomiting. Long curved sticks or carved manatee ribs were used for this. Figure 5.2 shows two views of the carved end of one of these vomiting sticks.

- One of the vessel types most closely identified with the Chican Ostionoid subseries and with the designation "Taíno" generally are large effigy vessels. These are sculpted in to human figures and large, ornate bottles (Figures 5.3 and 5.4). McGinnis's database has 61 from Hispaniola and only 1 from Puerto Rico.
- Another interesting contrast has to do with the circular stone "collars" or "ball belts" – among the most impressive and finely worked artifacts from the Caribbean (Figure 5.5). It is probably legitimate to link their use with the ball game although they and other related artifacts are powerful symbols of chiefly power

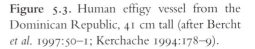

Figure 5.3. Human effigy vessel from the Dominican Republic, 41 cm tall (after Bercht *et al.* 1997:50–1; Kerchache 1994:178–9).

(Walker 1993). McGinnis recorded only 4 of the collars on Hispaniola that were carved with decorations (2 slender and 2 medium) and 79 from Puerto Rico (51 slender and 28 medium or massive).

- A range of artifacts is associated with chiefly burial, such as large urns or notched bowls are found on Hispaniola, but are absent on Puerto Rico. McGinnis records 19 high-status burial urns on Hispaniola, but no comparable ones for Puerto Rico.

There are other comparisons of this nature that can be made, but the point is that what we think of as "Taíno" culture has a considerable degree of variability, which can be seen in both the archaeological and ethnohistorical data (Alegría 1976). In the case of the evidence just reviewed, I believe it argues that the nature of polities and chiefship was different on the two islands. On Puerto Rico there was greater emphasis on the ball game and community ritual, and on Hispaniola corresponding importance was accorded to high-status individuals and their personal connections to powerful *cemís* and the spirit world. Although it is speculative, it is possible to

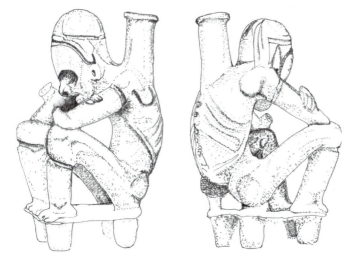

Figure 5.4. Human effigy vessel from the Dominican Republic, 24 cm tall, Fundación García Arévalo (after Kerchache 1994:170–3).

imagine the elites of Puerto Rico, in their beautiful houses with their finely wrought stone collars and surrounded by their complexes of ceremonial plazas, looking down on the relative upstarts from the neighboring island. They might have thought that on Hispaniola everything is bigger, brasher, richer, less subtle, more ostentatious, more dangerous, and in every way less connected with the ancient ways and aesthetics of at least some of their ancestors. Another way to see this difference, perhaps from the opposite perspective, is that

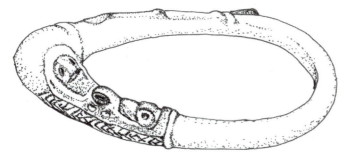

Figure 5.5. Stone belt or collar from Puerto Rico, 44 cm, Musée de l'Homme, Paris (after Bercht *et al.* 1997:plate 57).

the elites of Hispaniola were less constrained by tradition and more easily able to improvise and invent in spectacular ways.

As further evidence for the heterogeneity of late prehistoric societies, there is also considerable archaeological variability within the late ceramics on the island of Hispaniola itself. Veloz Maggiolo (1972:98–108) describes four ceramic styles – Macao, Meillac, Boca Chica, and Carrier – that reflect relatively distinct local traditions and developments. He acknowledges the complexity of the situation, however, noting that, "it is clear that in many occasions one style penetrates into the area of another" (1972:102). He further observes that the limited amount of archaeological work done to date gives us incomplete understanding of these stylistic regions and their intersections.

From the descriptions of the early European colonists on Hispaniola we get a more fine-grained insight into the situation in the late fifteenth century. In particular, it is clear that several languages were spoken on Hispaniola and that people in different regions had different histories and thought of themselves as culturally distinct. Bartolomé de Las Casas described the languages of Hispaniola in his *Historia de las Indias*:

> There were three distinct languages in this island, which were mutually unintelligible: the first was of the people we called the Lower Macorix, and the other of the people of Upper Macorix. . . . The other language was the universal one for all of the land, and was the most elegant and contained the most words, and was the most sweet in sound. Of the latter the speech of Xaraguá, as I have said earlier, carried the greatest prestige and was the main dialect. (Las Casas 1967 III:311)

Peter Martyr also comments on the linguistic diversity of Hispaniola:

> The cantons of the province of Hubabo are Xamana, Canabaco, Cubao, and others whose names I do not know. The cantons of Magua and Cacacubana belong to the province of Cahibo. The natives in this province speak an entirely different language from that spoken by the other islanders; they are called Macoryzes. In the canton of Cubana another language resembling none of the others is spoken; it is likewise used in the canton of Baiohaigua. (Martyr 1912 I:367–8)

A final interesting suggestion of linguistic diversity comes from Julian Granberry's article "Was Ciguayo a West Indian Hokan language?" (1991). Although he makes it clear that the article is speculative and based on sparse linguistic data, Granberry finds closer linguistic relatives for Ciguayo among Central American languages – where it is thought the earliest preceramic people came from – than in the Caribbean or northeastern South America (Granberry and Vescelius 2004).

On both Hispaniola and Cuba there are some historical references to people who were apparently hunter-gatherers who lived in the western extremities of each island. On Hispaniola, Martyr describes people on the southwestern peninsula of Haiti:

> who live only in caverns and eat nothing but the products of the forest. They have never been civilised nor had any inter-course with any other races of men. They live, so it is said, as people did in the golden age, without fixed homes or crops or culture; neither do they have a definite language. (Martyr 1912 I:380)

That report almost mirrors Las Casas's description of the people of far western Cuba. He said there were

> Indians at the Cape of Cuba [Cabo San Antonio] who are like savages, have no relations whatever with others of the island, nor do they have houses, but they live in caves, except when they go out to fish, and are called Guanahacabibes. (quoted in Sauer 1966:184)

Other names for this group (or groups) in western Cuba are the Gua-nahatabeys and Ciboneys (Rouse 1992:19–21). Bill Keegan (1989) has challenged the existence of these groups, noting that some of the early chroniclers had not been to the areas they were describing and also citing archaeological evidence for the presence of sedentary villages in these areas. In the case of southwestern Haiti, Las Casas himself refuted claims that hunter-gatherers lived there: "they only live in towns here and have their leaders who rule them, in the way of the others [Hispaniolan Taínos]" (quoted in Loven 1935:5–6). He mentions others on the tip of the peninsula who may have hidden themselves there to escape the Spanish and to avoid being forced into *encomiendas*.

At present, it seems that neither the archaeological evidence nor the ethnohistorical accounts can be definitive on this issue. Although there are archaeological sites in both southwestern Haiti and far western Cuba with evidence sedentary horticulture, pottery making, and so on, there are also late hunter-gatherer sites in the same area, and people employing these two economic strategies certainly could have lived side by side (Febles *et al.* 1995). Whether these hunter-gatherer groups were really there at the time of European conquest, it is clear that the neighboring people *thought* they were and described them to the Europeans. It could be that their presence was just a memory or that they were considered by their neighbors to be ethnically Guanahatabey, Guanahacabibe, or Ciboney, even though their economy and material culture may have been indistinguishable by that time.

CULTURAL DIVERSITY AND POLITICAL GEOGRAPHY IN THE LESSER ANTILLES

In spring 2003, André Delpuech and Corinne Hofman hosted a meeting in Leiden and Paris that resulted in a volume titled *Late Ceramic Age Societies in the Eastern Caribbean* (2004, B.A.R. International Series). The contributors to that volume spent several days discussing the late prehistory of the Lesser Antilles and the relationship between those islands and the Greater Antilles from about A.D. 800 onward. Although the authors speak for themselves in the collected volume, there was some degree of consensus around the following view of the later prehistory of the Lesser Antilles.

In the last few centuries before the arrival of Europeans, there was a great deal of interaction between the Windward Islands and the South American mainland. There had always been contact between the two areas, and the people of the Lesser Antilles were originally from the mainland, but the interaction intensified after about A.D. 1400 and continued into historic times (Hulme and Whitehead 1992; Whitehead 1988). When the French started to colonize Guadeloupe and some of the other islands in the 1630s, missionaries lived among the indigenous people and wrote some of the best ethnographic accounts we have of the people of the Caribbean (e.g., Breton 1892; Du Tertre 1667; Hulme and Whitehead 1992; Labat 1642). They documented the coming and going of people from and to the mainland and provided a great deal of insight into the social and political organization of the people, whom they called Caraïbes.

Raymond Breton was a missionary friar who went to the West Indies in 1635. His account of the origins of the Caraïbes (or Island Caribs) captures the way people felt about these mainland connections:

> Nothing can be learned from collecting all their dreams and fables touching upon their origin except that they are descended from closely neighbouring peoples of the islands who came from the mainland. This much is completely certain. The friendship that they have with them and the trade of the one with the other are some indication as well as the uniformity of the name by which they call themselves, namely *kallinago* following the language of men and *kalliponam* following the language of women; although, for some distinction among themselves and those of the mainland, they call the latter *Balouöouri*, from the word *Ballouö*, which means the mainland, as one would say a Parisian Frenchmen, or of *Langrois*. Thus they say a *kallinago* of the mainland. We call those from the mainland who are friends of our savages *Gallybis* and our savages *Caraïbes*.
>
> If you ask them how they derived from them and were carried over into the islands, they will not be able to give a reason for it. Duly, they all say that their first father Kallinago, having left the mainland accompanied by his family, set up home on Dominica. (quoted in Hulme and Whitehead 1992:108)

Reports of this nature, and the stories told by the people of the Greater Antilles and northern Lesser Antilles to early European observers, led the Europeans to envision a Carib invasion that was proceeding up through the island chain at the time of European contact. Sven Loven summed it up in the early twentieth century as follows: "According to all that we can learn from historical sources, we can conclude that the Taínos and Igneris lived [in the Caribbean] otherwise undisturbed, until the Calinas [Caribs] from the coast of

Guiana captured the Lesser Antilles from the Igneris and began their raids against the Taínos on the Greater Antilles and Bahamas" (Loven 1935:51).

A lot of scholarship over the last 20 years has centered on whether this view – of a late and widespread Carib migration into the archipelago – is completely accurate (see, e.g., Allaire 1996, 1997; Keegan 1996). There does not seem to be a body of archaeological evidence that matches the historical scenario. Archaeologists have not been able to identify some unique sort of Island Carib ceramics, for instance, which might serve as a marker of this migration. Instead, there is a better argument for continuity in the ceramic tradition, albeit with some evidence for late ceramics that have stylistic connections to the mainland (Allaire 1997; Boomert 1986; Rouse 1992). The widespread pottery found in the Windward Islands from about 1000 and afterward is called Suazoan Troumassoid by Rouse, after the site of Savannah Suazey on Grenada (Allaire 1991). The scenario that seems most likely at present is that there was considerable trade, interaction, and movement between long-resident Lesser Antillean populations and the people of the mainland and that through the generations, this interaction brought about cultural change and some degree of cultural synthesis between the islanders and the people from the mainland. What emerged from this prolonged interaction was a new cultural identity which the French missionaries described as Caraïbe or Island Carib.

The island of Guadeloupe seems to be a sort of threshold in the political geography of the archipelago in later prehistory. It is the northern extent of the distribution of Suazey ceramics, and beyond, to the northwest, where the archaeological evidence, particularly the ceramics, share similarities with the other Leeward Islands and to a great extent with Puerto Rico. The Leewards' connection with Puerto Rico seems most evident from around A.D. 800 to 1300. There are ceramic similarities between the Leeward Islands artifacts and the pottery of the Greater Antilles, and Puerto Rico seems to be the source of a lot of the exotic stone in the Leewards.

By around A.D. 1300 there is also some evidence for a Taíno interest or presence far out into the Leeward Islands. Hofman and Hoogland (Hofman and Hoogland 2005) have found substantial quantities of pottery with clear affinities to Chican ceramics of Hispaniola and Puerto Rico at the site of Kelby's Ridge site on Saba. Kelby's Ridge is high up on the mountain and relatively inaccessible and has a commanding view over the sea and islands in the Leeward chain to the east of Saba. The view of the sea to the east may have been one of the main reasons it was situated where it was. Crock and Petersen (2004) have also argued for Taíno influence and perhaps involvement in the northern Leeward Islands of Anguilla and St. Martin, and similar evidence comes from Nevis (Wilson 2006). Louis Allaire (1990) has even found evidence for a Taíno presence as far south as Martinique, more than 600 km southeastward from the coast of Puerto Rico.

Perhaps related to this apparent Taíno interest in the islands to the east, there is evidence that many of the Leeward Islands were either abandoned or very sparsely populated after around A.D. 1300 (Wilson 2006). The islands from Saba to Nevis, and perhaps the rest of the Leewards as well, seem to have been abandoned, at least for periods of time. It is plausible that an antagonistic relationship had developed between the people of the Windward Islands and those to the west of Guadeloupe. Perhaps it is related to the evidence for Taíno influence and interest in the region (as seen at Kelby's Ridge on Saba). For whatever reason, it seems that the Leeward Islands were not a safe place to be after around A.D. 1300.

Crock and Peterson (2004) have argued that prior to around A.D. 1300, the Leeward Islands communities were sustained by a highly interactive trade network that linked the dozen or so islands between Montserrat and the Virgin Islands. Menno Hoogland (personal communication, 2003) has argued that such a network would have been essential to the survival of individual communities and has suggested that if the network collapsed, or if parts of the region were abandoned, the others may have had to leave as well. The idea that there was a relatively depopulated buffer zone in the northern Caribbean in late prehistory is very intriguing, and hopefully it will be the focus of additional research in the future.

Until the 1990s, a significant gap in our knowledge of Caribbean archaeology involved the later prehistory of the large Windward Islands from Guadeloupe south. These islands were the focus of a good deal of archaeological research in the 1960s and 1970s, but there had been a diminution in research after that. Now a good deal of research is being carried out by the French Service Régional de l'Archéologie on Guadeloupe and Martinique, and exciting research is underway on several other islands. Keegan, Hofman, and Hoogland (2002) have undertaken a multiyear program of research on St. Lucia that is just beginning to be published. Richard Callaghan has also begun a multiyear project on St. Vincent. Other archaeologists are also carrying out new research in the region (e.g., Delpuech, Hofman and Hoogland 2003).

TRAJECTORIES OF CHANGE ON THE EVE OF EUROPEAN CONTACT

The arrival of Europeans set into motion a series of disasters for the indigenous people of the Caribbean. In the Greater Antilles, disease, economic disruption, famine, and forced labor demands combined to bring about precipitous population loss and the disintegration of the Taíno sociopolitical systems (Anderson-Córdova 1990; Wilson 1990). The people of the Lesser Antilles fared somewhat better, in part because the real conquest of those islands did not take place until the 1620s. Also, as will be discussed in Chapter 6, population densities were lower in the Lesser Antilles, and epidemics were thus not quite so catastrophic as they were on the larger islands (Cook and Borah 1971; Rey 1988; Wilson 1997). In neither the Greater nor the Lesser Antilles were the indigenous populations completely destroyed. They survived in both areas and became part of the subsequent colonial population, with its mix of people from Africa, Europe, Asia, and elsewhere in the Americas.

The events of the early contact period are affected by the trajectories of change that were established in the centuries before contact. These patterns of change are certainly part of the story of what was happening in the Caribbean in late prehistory and help us to understand the archaeological and historical evidence we have.

One important trajectory of change in later prehistory was the expansionism being exhibited by the larger Taíno polities. This trend is reflected in the growth of political entities in Cuba, Jamaica, the Bahamas, and the Virgin Islands that are very much like those found in Hispaniola and Puerto Rico. The early chroniclers commented on this when in Cuba. Las Casas viewed the Cuban elites, who held other Cubans in a state of subjugation, to be recent arrivals in the island: "We believe it hasn't been 50 years since those from that island [Hispaniola] came to settle on Cuba" (cited in Loven 1935:69). Similarly, Rouse sees clear archaeological evidence for people from Hispaniola migrating to the southern coast of Puerto Rico (1986:148–9). This apparently took place with enough time for some of the stylistic characteristics of the Chican pottery to be adopted by their Puerto Rican neighbors.

And as noted, we see an archaeological presence far down the Lesser Antillean chain, certainly through the Leeward Islands and possibly down the Windward Islands as well. This evidence is widely scattered but generally not intensive. Apart from Kelby's Ridge on Saba, which may be an outpost of some sort, most of the other finds are isolated pieces – perhaps symbolic objects, gifts, or rare trade goods.

There is some evidence of interaction between the Greater Antilles and the mainland, particularly with the Yucatan Peninsula and the areas that are now Nicaragua, Costa Rica, and Panama. On his first voyage Columbus saw beehives and honey on Cuba, but apparently the species of bee and the practice of keeping bees for their honey and wax originated in the Yucatan (Loven 1935:59; Veloz Maggiolo 1972:111). During the early years of the Spanish presence around the Yucatan, at least one canoe full of people, reportedly from Jamaica, showed up at the island of Cozumel. In terms of similarities in artifacts between the Antilles and Central America there are several possibilities (Wilson 2005), but in many cases there are significant questions about the original provenance of the artifacts and their date of discovery.

At a stylistic level, McGinnis argues for ideographic influence from Central America in the Greater Antilles. She notes,

> It is in the category of ceremonial weapons that the influence of the Isthmian mainland on Hispaniola artifacts is easiest to see. Hispaniola ceremonial axes, celts, and daggers all appear very similar to such objects found in what is now Costa Rica. Some of them are almost identical. (personal communication, 2004)

As Veloz Maggiolo (1972:108–15) and others have argued, this is a question that deserves to be taken seriously, even with the difficulties in reaching sound interpretations of the archaeological evidence for long distance contact. It is not difficult, however, to imagine what might have motivated Caribbean people to make such long voyages, even though they had a small tangible result in terms of the movement of people or goods. In her book *Ulysses' Sail* (1988), Mary Helms explores the connection between geographical distance and the kinds of esoteric knowledge that were so important in establishing the legitimacy of chiefs. She describes the wide-ranging journeys of young elites gaining experience and special kinds of knowledge:

> To the extent (and it varies greatly among societies) that geographically distant places, peoples, and experiences are perceived (either at first hand or by some manner of extrapolation) within essentially supernatural or cosmological contexts, then knowledge of, or acquaintance with, geographically distant places, peoples, and things rightfully falls within the domain of political-religious specialists whose job it is to deal with "mysteries." Knowledge of geographically distant phenomena, whether acquired directly or indirectly, may be expected for form part of the corpus of esoteric knowledge controlled by these traditional specialists, even as esoteric knowledge of "vertical" or "other" dimensions of the sacred falls within their domain. Stated somewhat differently, the select few who are either able or expected to become familiar with geographically distant phenomena may be accorded an aura of prestige and awe approaching the same order, if not always the same magnitude, as that accorded political religious specialists or elites in general. (Helms 1988:5)

In her book *Ancient Panama*, Helms (1979:176) describes young Panamanian rulers traveling to South America to "confer with elite leaders of recognized intellectual excellence" and there acquiring the esoteric knowledge that set them apart from their competitors. In the case of Panama this travel may be reflected in the archaeological record by the presence of goods from Colombia and elsewhere, but from ethnohistoric records and ethnographies, it is clear that the most important things they brought back were the songs, dances, verbal performances, and other forms of special knowledge. Distance helped imbue this knowledge with special power.

In the Caribbean, the archaeological evidence is not strong enough to make a solid case for sustained cultural interaction between the Greater Antilles and the mainland. Nevertheless, it is likely that such voyages were happening in late prehistory, further suggesting that the Taíno polities were reaching out in all directions, expanding their sphere of knowledge and influence.

SUMMARY

On the eve of European arrival Caribbean people were already in the midst of a period of change as profound as they had undergone in the preceding five millennia. The relative stability that had characterized many earlier periods had given way to change as new sociopolitical institutions emerged and sought to extend their influence into other regions and islands. *Cacicazgos* on Hispaniola were growing in size and influence and competing with each other for territory, population, and status (Cassá 1974 Charlevoix 1731–1733; Nau 1894). So the political situation the first Europeans entered was an unstable and dangerous one.

It was also a period of artistic fluorescence. On Hispaniola and throughout the Greater Antilles, Taíno art was flamboyant and original with extraordinary sculptural creations in stone (Figure 5.6), ceramics, and wood, as well as elaborate works in beads, cotton, and basketry (Bercht *et al.* 1997). On Puerto Rico carved stonework was as refined, delicate, and detailed as any in the Americas (Kerchache 1994).

The situation in the Lesser Antilles was also in flux. There, too, the political geography was shifting as connections with the mainland grew in importance. New groups from the mainland may have been moving into the archipelago (Allaire 1996; Boomert 1986), and interaction with people from the Greater Antilles may have caused settlement changes in the Leeward Islands.

What would have happened if Europeans had not come? Probably the situation would have gone on with continued or even accelerated

Figure 5.6. Stone sculpture from the Dominican Republic, length 25 cm, height 19 cm (after Bercht *et al.* 1997:plates 9–11).

change, with additional political integration and additional conflict. It is also likely that there would have been greater interactions with the surrounding mainlands – South America, lower Central America, the Yucatan, and Florida (Bullen and Sleight 1963; Keegan 1987).

CHAPTER 6

THE CARIBBEAN AFTER THE ARRIVAL OF EUROPEANS

In the autumn of 1492, a small fleet of three ships crossed the Atlantic Ocean, carried along by the north equatorial current and the trade winds. They were looking for a direct route to China and Japan, where they hoped to trade for silks, porcelain, and other exotic goods that until then had been carried by caravan along the ancient Silk Road. They sought a new route that avoided the Near East and Constantinople, because that city (by then called Istanbul) was now under the control of the Ottoman Empire (Wilson 1999).

These explorers made landfall in the Bahamas and spent a little time there interacting with the people they met. Eventually they concluded that more populous and potentially richer trading areas lay to the south. They had read accounts of east Asia by Marco Polo and others, but the people they met in the Bahamas did not really match their expectations. Certainly they didn't have the large cities and golden palaces described by Marco Polo, but maps of the day showed dozens of islands around Cipangu or Japan, so the explorers reasoned that they were still on the peripheries of the famous kingdoms (Martin Behaim's maps and globes were among the best until 1492; see Ravenstein 1908; Wilson 1999:33–40). They set off to the south, stopping at several islands to take possession of them, trade, and take on fresh water. In this way they made their way down the archipelago, still searching for cities.

Along the way, just three days after they had first made their first landfall, the explorers had a significant encounter at sea. They came upon a lone man in a small canoe, out in the open sea between the Bahamian islands (Dunn and Kelley's 1989 translation of Columbus's journal of his first voyage, p. 85). The Europeans pulled the man and his canoe aboard their ship and took stock of his possessions – a calabash of water, a fist-sized piece of cassava bread, and a hard paste of red ochre pigment wrapped in leaves, used for body painting and ceramic decoration. The pigment was something of value, because others had offered it to the Europeans in trade for beads, coins, hawk's bells, clothes, and other goods. The man in the canoe also had a small basket and in it a small string of glass beads and two blancas or small-denomination coins. These European objects made it clear that news of the strange visitors was spreading before them as they went through the islands, and after that they met very few people who weren't already aware of their coming.

The small fleet made its way south and eventually crossed over to the northwest coast of Cuba. There they did see larger villages, with larger houses and more gold. They saw even more people on the eastern tip of Cuba and in Western Hispaniola. Here is Bartolomé de Las Casas's copy of Columbus's description of the landscape he saw as he was traveling east across the north coast of Haiti:

> The big island appears to be very high land not closed in by mountains, but level like handsome and extensive farmland; and all, or a large part of it, appeared to be cultivated, and the planted fields looked like wheat in the month of May in the farmlands of Cordova. They saw many fires that night and, by day, much smoke like signals that seemed to be warnings of some people with whom they were at war. All the coast of this land goes to the east. (Dunn and Kelley 1989:203)

Along the same coast a few days later, the explorers described a large village:

> These men went to the village, which was four and a half leagues to the southeast, and which they found in a very great valley. [It was] empty because, when they heard the Christians coming, all of the Indians fled inland leaving everything that they had. The village was of a thousand houses and of more than three thousand inhabitants. (Dunn and Kelley 1989:221)

Figure 6.1. An elite structure from Gonzalo Fernández de Oviedo y Valdés's (1959) manuscript of the *Historia General y Natural de las Indias* (1539–1548). The door suggests the scale of the building. Ethnohistoric accounts describe groups of 80–100 people gathering in similar buildings.

In these early encounters and in the first few years of the conquest of the Caribbean, the Europeans learned of the scale and nature of the Taíno societies. They learned that there was a series of polities that interacted with one another but were generally autonomous. Some of these were large, incorporating tens of thousands of people, and some were smaller, encompassing just a group of villages or a valley (Cassá 1974; Keegan *et al.* 1998; Vega 1980; Wilson 1990).

The Europeans encountered a society that was structured in ways that for the most part made sense to them. There were identifiable social strata with elites, commoners, and slaves. There were religious specialists and political leaders with obvious authority (Figures 6.1 and 6.2 show elite houses; they are are from Gonzalo Fernández de Oviedo y Valdés's (1959) manuscript of the *Historia General y Natural de las Indias* [1539–1548]). The status-conscious Europeans could easily discern who was at the top of the status hierarchy (although in this they were wrong because the highest status people in this matrilineal society were women, not the powerful men who ruled for them).

Columbus's description of his first encounter with such a *cacique* (chief) reflected each participant's understanding of the other's status.

> All of the Indians returned with the Christians to the village, which he affirms to be the largest and the best arranged with streets than any other of those passed through and found up to that time. . . . Until then the Admiral had not been able to understand whether cacique meant king or governor [*rey* or *gobernador*]. They also use another name for an important person, whom they call *nitayno*. He does not know if they say it for noble, or governor, or judge. Finally the cacique came to them and the whole town, more than two thousand persons, gathered in the plaza, which was well swept. This king was very courteous to the people from the ships, and each of the common people brought them something to eat and drink. Afterward the king gave to each one some of the pieces of cotton cloth that the women wear, and parrots for the Admiral, and certain pieces of gold. (Dunn and Kelley 1989:271)

The Europeans' understandings of the Taíno world changed with greater experience. More islanders learned to speak the European languages used by those who soon became conquerors rather than explorers. Many Europeans learned the languages spoken in the Caribbean, and commented in greater detail about the customs and cosmologies of the people they met (e.g., Arrom 1997; Pané 1974). With experience came better understanding of the languages spoken in the islands (Granberry and Vescelius 2004; Highfield 1997), as well as the social organization (Keegan 1997) and economy of the islanders (Peterson 1997).

SOCIOPOLITICAL AND DEMOGRAPHIC CONSEQUENCES OF EUROPEAN CONTACT

The impact of European conquest on the indigenous populations of the Caribbean was horrific. Within 30 years the population had decreased by more than 90% (Henige 1978). The main cause of the population collapse was the spread of catastrophic diseases, probably including smallpox, measles, influenza, and yellow fever (Crosby

Figure 6.2. Another form of elite architecture depicted by Oviedo.

1975; Dobyns 1976, 1983:257–8; Ramenofsky 1987). It is likely that in the Greater Antilles more than 80% of the population died of epidemic diseases. In many cases, people became sick and died without ever having seen a European, because like the coins and beads in the canoe stopped by Columbus, the pathogens dispersed out ahead of the conquistadores themselves.

The impact of European diseases throughout the Americas was terrible (Dobyns 1983). For many centuries Europe had been both a breeding ground for new epidemic diseases and the site of repeated epidemics that began elsewhere. French social historian Le Roy Ladurie has called Europe a "common market of microbes" because of the series of epidemics that raged through the European populace from the Middle Ages onward (Le Roy Ladurie 1981:30). Diseases came to Europe from distant Asia along the Silk Road and from sub-Saharan Africa via caravan traders. Repeated epidemics came through Europe, for example, the ruinous outbreaks of bubonic plague in the sixth century, the Black Death of the fourteenth century, and continuing outbreaks of plague in the fifteenth through twentieth centuries (Diamond 1999; Orent 2004). Europe was never completely free of new strains and varieties of measles, contagious fevers, and the myriad influenza viruses that pass back and forth between humans and their domesticated animals.

A second important factor in the population collapse in the Caribbean was starvation brought about by economic disruption (Anderson Córdova 1990; Wilson 1990:74–110). Cassava, the most important staple crop, took a long time to mature, and after harvesting some roots, others had to be replanted almost continuously. If the *conucos* (cultivation plots) were not replanted because of the disruptive impact of the epidemics, or because many people were pressed into service for mining or other reasons, the supply of cassava would eventually run out (Sauer 1966).

Despite the epidemics and enforced labor demands of the Spanish, the indigenous people of the Caribbean resisted conquest and fought to maintain their lands, sovereignty, and independence. Initially they sought alliances with the Spaniards, but when the foreign presence came to number in the many hundreds, and their demands grew so great, the Taíno organized armed uprising. In 1497, in the interior valley of Hispaniola, Columbus's brother Bartolomé and his forces narrowly avoided battle with as many as 15,000 Taíno warriors (Wilson 1990:74–110). Smaller skirmishes were frequent on Hispaniola, Cuba, Jamaica, and Puerto Rico (Anderson-Córdova 1989; de Herrera [Peguero 1975]; Moya Pons 1983; Southey 1827). Resistance took other forms as well, generally aimed at avoiding conscription for forced labor, maintaining Taíno social and political order, and continuing Taíno religious practice (Anderson Córdova 1989:106–33).

Karen Anderson-Córdova shows that the contact period and the process of Indian acculturation on Hispaniola and Puerto Rico were very complex. Large numbers of Indians were brought to the islands as slaves, and some indigenous people managed to leave the Greater Antilles. She estimates that by the time of the *Repartimiento* of 1514 (a process of assigning forced laborers to particular Europeans), about 30% of the Indians of Hispaniola and Puerto Rico were from elsewhere. They were brought from the Bahamas, Lesser Antilles, and northern South America, but they also came from as far away as Florida and Brazil (Anderson-Córdova 1989:218–75).

So Hispaniola and Puerto Rico had two populations of indigenous people – the Taíno people from the islands and Indians brought from elsewhere. Anderson-Córdova suggests that the enslaved Indians who came from other islands or the mainland had to adapt and assimilate more quickly than the Taíno did to survive, because the Taíno were allowed to remain in their own villages under a system she terms "compartmentalization" (1990:290–1). Under that system the Taíno accommodated the Spaniards to the extent they had to but maintained their own way of life in villages. The mortality rate, however, was still very high and these villages were losing population rapidly. They also fled from their islands into the Lesser Antilles and beyond, further diminishing the population (Anderson-Córdova 1990:218–75).

The cultural situation in the Greater Antilles in the first decades after conquest was complex, marked by the interactions of many different Indian and African groups, as well as diverse Europeans. Within this multicultural milieu, the indigenous people of the islands did not all perish. Indeed there is evidence that some survived by assimilating into the new colonial society (Floyd 1973; Nau 1894; Wilson 1997a, 1997b). The 1530 census on Puerto Rico shows that intermarriage between Europeans and Indians was not unusual, and many Indians were free of forced labor (Anderson-Córdova 1990:181–6). Archaeological remains supports this view of some degree of Taíno continuity as well; Kathleen Deagan (2004) has recently argued persuasively that although the archaeological evidence in historical sites for the persistence of an indigenous presence requires care to recover and identify, it is certainly there.

CULTURE CONTACT IN THE LESSER ANTILLES

In the Lesser Antilles the history of European contact differed significantly from the Greater Antilles. From the second voyage of Columbus onward, most trans-Atlantic voyages made landfall in the Lesser Antilles. Many ships coming from Europe landed at Martinique, Dominica, and Guadeloupe and spent some time taking on fresh water, fuel wood, and food and trading with the people there (Southey 1827). As a result of that contact, epidemic diseases swept through these populations as well, carried from island to island. Via indigenous routes of trade and interaction, diseases also spread into the South American interior (Whitehead 1988). But the historical evidence suggests that in the islands the impact of these epidemics was not as devastating as it was in the Greater Antilles (Wilson 1997b). Villages were smaller, more widely separated, and more independent. And although people, goods, and information flowed up and down the archipelago, there were some cultural barriers and historical animosities that may have acted as barriers to the spread of disease as well. As noted in Chapter 5, for example, there may have been a buffer zone in the eastern Leeward Islands between two groups.

In general, then, the impact of Europeans in the Lesser Antilles came from five kinds of interactions. The first was the kind of contact just mentioned, between the crews of ships making landfall and trading with local inhabitants.

The second dramatic kind of interaction came when disease, famine, and overwork had reduced the populations of the Greater Antilles to a point where more laborers were needed. Slave raids were carried out in the Lesser Antilles to capture workers for the gold mines of the Greater Antilles (Floyd 1973; Sued Badillo 1978, 1983). The raids were soon met with armed resistance, but still many people were taken from the islands or driven into hiding or flight to other islands. This practice also accounts for much of the depopulation of Jamaica, Cuba, and the Bahamas (Keegan 1992, 1997b).

Third, trading relations changed in parts of the islands as a result of Spanish influence and power. Before conquest, there was a pattern of interaction between the Lesser Antilles and Puerto Rico that included trade, sharing of resources, and sometimes raiding. There is, for example, evidence that people from the Lesser Antilles had an arrangement to come to Puerto Rico for canoe-sized trees. In one account from southeast Puerto Rico, people identified as "Caribs" killed the *cacique* of a coastal village. According to Peter Martyr's accounts from the early contact period (1970:259), "[The perpetrators] alleged that this cacique had violated the laws of hospitality in his relations with several Caribs, who were boat-builders. These men had been left at [Puerto Rico] to build more canoes, since that island grows lofty trees, better adapted for canoe building than those of the island of Santa Cruz [St. Croix]." The European presence eventually disrupted or destroyed regional trading systems up and down the archipelago.

A fourth form of interaction was raiding and warfare, initiated both from the Lesser Antilles toward Puerto Rico and other European settlements and from Europeans against the villages and people of the Lesser Antilles. From early in the occupation of Puerto Rico, tremendous animosity developed between the Spaniards and people from the Lesser Antilles. Contemporary accounts describe raids that hit settlements in Puerto Rico almost continuously from the time of the earliest Spanish colonization. Raids are reported in 1508, 1509, 1515, 1521, 1528–1532, 1538, and 1547, and it is likely that many escaped official record (Southey 1827; Tapía y Rivera 1945). Numerous petitions were filed between 1528 and 1532 by local Spaniards demanding that armed vessels and men be provided to cruise against the people of the Lesser Antilles. Such a retaliatory voyage had been undertaken around 1510 and subsequently raids diminished. Spanish attacks carried out especially in the Virgin and Leeward Islands after 1532 were particularly devastating (Southey 1827:163), totally depopulating some of the islands: an attack on St. Croix in 1555 effectively ended the indigenous occupation of the island.

A final general pattern of interaction was one that helped the people of the Lesser Antilles to survive European contact and has allowed their descendants to survive to this day. There were mechanisms within Island Carib culture to incorporate and assimilate other people into their society. The Island Caribs effectively increased their numbers by taking captives while raiding and through the incorporation people who were shipwrecked or Africans escaping enslavement. An illuminating example of this can be seen in the case of Luisa de Navarette, who was captured by Island Caribs in a raid on Puerto Rico in 1576 and escaped and was interviewed about her experiences in 1580 (Hulme and Whitehead 1992:38–44, from the petition of Bernáldez de Quiroz).

Luisa de Navarette is described as "black skinned, a free ex-slave, and of good name and Spanish-speaking, and a resident of this city." She had been taken from the town of Humacao, on the southeastern corner of Puerto Rico, and transported to Dominica, nearly 600 km away (this gives an idea of the geographical scope of canoe travel and Island Carib raiding). She reported that her captors raided Puerto Rico yearly, and in these raids, "they have carried away a great quantity of negroes and left some in Dominica and distributed the rest amongst the Indians of these islands…" (Hulme and Whitehead 1992:40). There were an estimated 300 European and African captives on Dominica at the time, and many others on other islands, so Luisa de Navarette's story was not really unusual. Many captives were incorporated into Island Carib society. A report from St. Vincent that was written more than 100 years after the Luisa de Navarette account, in 1700 (by Intendant Robert, Hulme and Whitehead 1992:172–4), describes neighboring groups of *Caraïbes* and Africans – Africans whom Intendant Robert hoped to enslave and sell to French or Spanish colonies. He accounts for their presence there by noting that, "a long time before this a ship full of negroes wrecked and lost on the windward of St Vincent, many [of whom] were received kindly by the *Caraïbes*; it is this event that began settlement of these negroes on St Vincent, where they live" (Hulme and Whitehead 1992:173).

These five processes or patterns of interaction – ship-based trade, disease, slave raiding, interisland trading, raiding, and cultural adoption – help us understand the context and nature of cultural change in the nearly three centuries between Columbus's first voyage and the final treaties with the Island Caribs in the late 1700s.

INDIGENOUS RESISTENCE IN THE CARIBBEAN

A consistent indigenous response, from the earliest European contact in the Lesser Antilles to the final defeats of the indigenous people of the Caribbean, was resistance to European encroachment and conquest. In general, the islanders were willing to allow landings and trade and would allow Europeans to take on water and collect other resources, but they would resist with violence any attempts to establish permanent settlements or to take captives.

One of the first examples of resistance to colonization occurred in 1526, when Antonio Serrano led a Spanish attempt to colonize

Guadeloupe, the largest of the Lesser Antilles. In part he hoped to capitalize on the expansion of the Bishopric of San Juan granted by the Crown in 1519, expanding Spanish control eastward, and he also hoped to help pacify the people of the Lesser Antilles and reduce their raiding on Puerto Rico (Boromé 1966:32–3). This colonization attempt was quickly repelled. Earlier, Juan Ponce de León had tried to establish a temporary settlement on Guadeloupe in 1515 but was attacked by a large party and forced to retreat to Puerto Rico. He had to abandon many of his group who had been captured (Martyr 1970 I:401–3; Southey 1827I:122).

By 1550, English and French interest in the Caribbean was increasing. After a few small-scale attempts to participate in trade in the Spanish Caribbean or to capture vessels returning to Spain, English activity in the region increased dramatically in the 1580s and 1590s. Most of their expeditions were attacks on Spanish settlements and shipping, and the Lesser Antilles were convenient places to replenish their ships after the Atlantic crossing before moving on to the mainland coasts or the Greater Antilles. Sir Francis Drake, with a fleet of 25 vessels, raided in the Caribbean in 1585. He attacked in Spain and the Cape Verde Islands on his way west and then headed for the Caribbean. He burned Santo Domingo on Hispaniola and captured Cartagena and then went north to Florida and captured St. Augustine (Hakluyt 1904:Vol. X).

The English captain John White traded peacefully on Dominica in 1590, and his account was typical of most English interactions in the Lesser Antilles during this period: "The first of May in the morning many of the Salvages came aboord our ships in their canowes, and did traffique with us; we also the same day landed and entered their towne whence we returned the same day aboord without any resistance of the Salvages; or any offence done to them" (Burrage 1906:308). Between 1580 and 1600, many more or less peaceful English landfalls are recorded in the Lesser Antilles, and these continued into the 1600s.

When English parties attempted to colonize the Lesser Antilles, however, they were almost immediately resisted by the indigenous inhabitants. In 1605 Captain Nicholas St. John and 66 others, fearing that their ship could not make it back to England, resolved to colonize St. Lucia. For six weeks they were on relatively peaceful terms with the Island Caribs and one of their leaders, Augramert. Eventually, however, these peaceful relations broke down. A party including Captain Saint John went searching for gold in the interior of the island and never returned. Those who remained behind were attacked by a party of 300 Indians. Four days later 1,400 Island Caribs arrived by canoe from other islands. All but 19 of the Europeans were killed, and of them 12 were wounded. Some of the local Caribs brought them food, and a man named Antonie, reportedly Augramert's brother, traded them a canoe with which to flee. He told them that Augramert was coming from St. Vincent the next day with 12 canoes to finish them off (Southey 1827, I:236; Purchas 1905[1625] IV:1257). Another English group attempted to colonize Grenada in 1609, and the result was similar. Figure 6.3 shows the changing control of the islands of the Lesser Antilles in the seventeenth century, as island after island changed hands between the indigenous people and the Europeans.

On the southern end of the Lesser Antillean archipelago the indigenous people fought relentlessly to maintain possession of Tobago. Indeed, they fought more tenaciously there than they did in most other islands (Southey 1827). Tobago was the site of repeated colonization attempts by the Dutch, but all of the attempts were driven back. Battles were fought on Tobago in 1625, 1632, and 1642, and there were many other skirmishes. One possible explanation for why they fought so much harder for Tobago than, for example, Trinidad, was that Tobago may have been the more critical link between the Windward Isles and the mainland. As a stepping-stone to the mainland, it was the only way to maintain contact with affiliated groups there, and it was also the only route of retreat if they had to abandon the Lesser Antilles completely (Hulme 1986; Hulme and Whitehead 1992; Whitehead 1988).

Another factor in the battles over Tobago involves competition between European states. In the battles of 1632 and 1642, Island Caribs from the Lesser Antilles were assisted by Spaniards from Trinidad and the mainland in repelling Dutch colonization. The Spanish and the Island Caribs, who had been enemies for many generations, joined forces to hold Tobago. For the Island Caribs it was

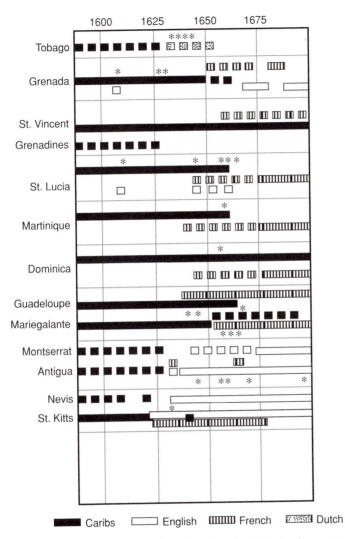

Figure 6.3. Chronological chart showing the shifts in the control of the Lesser Antilles in the seventeenth century. Asterisks mark major battles between indigenous people and Europeans.

probably to maintain the crucial link with the mainland; for the Spaniards, it was to limit the incursion of other European powers into what they saw as their own domain on the northeastern coast of South America.

These struggles for control of Tobago illuminate one of two strategies employed by the Island Caribs to prevent the further colonization of European powers. The Island Caribs would ally themselves with a European force who shared the aim of preventing the colonization of an island by another national group. The Spanish wanted to obstruct the English or Dutch colonization of Tobago, a desire shared by the Island Caribs of St. Vincent and Grenada (and certainly those of Tobago).

In another example, in 1653, a party of Island Caribs, assisted and encouraged by the French, traveled 200 km from Dominica to raid the English on Antigua. Here, the indigenous islanders allied themselves with the French, who had little desire to colonize Antigua. Both the French and the Caribs wanted to prevent the English from establishing themselves any further in the eastern Caribbean, and Antigua was the least well defended of the English islands at that time (Southey 1827, I:331; Du Tertre 1671 I:418). Over 20 years later the English feared this Carib-French alliance and remembered its impact:

> [T]he French drew them [the Island Caribs] to their assistance in the late war, and will again on occasion; and the [English] islanders dread them more than any other, because they can come with 30 or 40 periagoes [canoes] to windward, whilst they are at leeward in the trenches or opposing a landing Christian enemy, and so destroy men, women, and children, and burn all, as the people of Antigua and Montserrat have felt in the last war. (Calendar of State Papers 1889 VI:547)

The mid-1600s was a period of intensive European colonization efforts, and Island Carib resistance was gradually being overwhelmed. The islanders' contacts with the South American mainland which had existed prior to contact were severed by this time (Whitehead 1988). The Taíno populations of the Greater Antilles were almost completely decimated by this period, and interactions between the Greater and Lesser Antilles had ended a century before. The Island Caribs had been forced to abandon the Leeward Islands as well as the southern Windwards. By the 1650s the only islands permanently occupied by Caribs were St. Vincent, St.

Lucia, Martinique, Dominica, and Guadeloupe (Richardson 1992; Rogonzinski 2000).

In 1660 the French and Island Caribs signed a treaty that called for the cessation of all warfare and included an agreement by which the Caribs would maintain control of Dominica and St. Vincent. The agreement also called for the Island Caribs to allow French missionaries to live among them (Southey 1827, II:33; Du Tertre 1671). The most detailed ethnographic and linguistic observations we have come from these missionaries (Hulme and Whitehead 1992). By this time the Island Caribs had lost the ability to organize large-scale collective raids and to forge effective alliances with one European group against another. Their numbers, even augmented by the incorporation of captives and recruits, were not sufficient to overcome the strong defenses put up by the now-large European populations. This ended their ability to be an important ally to European powers or an effective military force in their own right.

The history of indigenous–European interaction from 1493 to 1700 demonstrates that the Island Caribs were active agents who exerted tremendous influence on the way European colonization proceeded in the Lesser Antilles. They played a crucial role in limiting Spanish colonization in the area. They manipulated relations between the English, Spanish, Dutch, French, and other European states to their own advantage, and ultimately they were able to negotiate a treaty that left them in partial control of Dominica and St. Vincent.

CHAPTER 7

CONCLUSIONS

Nearly 6,000 years ago, people began to move into the islands of the Caribbean archipelago from the surrounding mainlands. In subsequent millennia they followed a historical trajectory that in some ways paralleled events taking place elsewhere in the Americas. Ultimately, however, the human experience in the Caribbean was unique. The islands of the Caribbean were to a considerable extent a world set apart from the rest of the Americas – connected to wider historical currents but distinct and able to follow a different historical trajectory.

This volume has explored the archaeological evidence for the remarkable story of Caribbean prehistory. The story spans several millennia, hundreds of human generations, and includes periods of dramatic change as well as long periods of continuity. It has taken a century of work by a diverse and remarkable group of archaeologists to piece this story together to the extent that we know it. Yet even now it sometimes seems as if Caribbean archaeologists are working in *terra incognita*. Many islands lack basic inventories of archaeological sites, and on others only the largest and most obvious sites are well recorded. The past four centuries of intensive agriculture have brought about extensive landscape modifications that have erased much of this archaeological record, and the accelerating pace of coastal development for tourism is destroying more of the archaeological record year by year. Island governments are caught between the need to develop tourism, on one hand, and the desire to preserve their island's cultural heritage, on the other, and too often the forces pushing for development overwhelm local preservation efforts.

Although some islands and areas have received little archaeological attention, other areas are coming to be well understood through sustained programs of archaeological research in places such as Guadeloupe, Martinique, the U.S. Virgin Islands, Puerto Rico, and Cuba. Comprehensive archaeological surveys and the systematic testing of many sites are providing a body of data with which we can explore new kinds of questions. As the present volume has documented, much of the last century's archaeological research was focused on refining artifact chronologies, understanding migrations of peoples, and, to an extent, reconstructing economic strategies and adaptations. As a result of this work, the general outline of archaeological chronology is now relatively well known, although lacking in detail.

For each chronological period archaeologists have addressed different questions and in the process they have developed new insights. Here, we can review some of the major themes explored in this volume.

From the first migrations, the people of the Caribbean confronted new situations and invented new ways of relating to their physical and cultural environments. As discussed in Chapter 2, dealing with the first migrants to the islands, these early explorers encountered pristine environments that had never experienced human exploitation. They brought about the extinction of some endemic species and brought with them parts of the ecosystems they came from, including exotic plants and animals. In the end, they both adapted to their new setting and to an extent remade their new environment in ways that suited them.

From about 4000 B.C. to around 2000 B.C. and afterward, the Antilles were colonized from two directions – from the Yucatan to the west and from northeastern South America to the south. Neither migration was very large, and in neither case were their settlements very dense on the landscape. Both were successful, however. In their new settings generation after generation lived lives that were similar to those of their parents and grandparents, hunting, fishing, and collecting in the rich terrestrial environments as well as the abundant littoral, reef, and ocean environments. Trade goods such as high-quality chert were traded widely and communities stayed in touch through time over long distances.

The two groups of preceramic Caribbean people eventually encountered one another somewhere in the eastern Greater Antilles or northern Lesser Antilles. Although their ways of relating to the landscape were similar, their histories, languages, and cultures were very different. It was the first time substantially different groups came into direct contact in the Caribbean. It is unfortunately the case that we do not know enough about the lives of either of these groups. An important research direction for the future is to understand them better and to find ways to illuminate this early period of culture contact.

In the last 500 years B.C., people in the Lesser Antilles and Puerto Rico began another period of culture contact and change as new migrants from South America explored the archipelago and set up colonies. As discussed in Chapter 3, this Saladoid phenomenon initially looked to archaeologists like the rapid influx of a new group of people – sedentary horticulturalists who brought their manioc-based economy with them from the lowlands of South America. Now the process looks more complex, with multiple early attempts, abandoned efforts, and lost colonies and probably several areas of origin on the mainland. This migration also involved the interaction of people with different cultures and economies, as the Saladoid people moved into islands long occupied by others. Again, we know frustratingly little about their relations. Were the original islanders driven out? Were they incorporated within Saladoid society or did they both occupy the same islands without conflict? As discussed in Chapter 3, researchers are beginning to see that the situation may have involved each of these scenarios to some extent, in ways that probably went on for many centuries.

Caribbean prehistory seems to have more than its share of migrations, cultural interaction, and culture change, and these processes are crucial to understanding the past in this region. To understand the nuances of migration and cultural interaction and change, it has grown more and more apparent that we must be sensitive to extremely subtle aspects of the archaeological record. In the case of the Saladoid migration, a technological change like the use of pottery is obvious, but was this change accompanied by changes in lithic technology, foodways, inter- and intrasite settlement patterns, trade, and social organization? Does it reflect a replacement of one group by another or a complex synthesis of multiple groups and practices? As archaeologists throughout the world are learning, understanding these dynamics requires extremely close analysis of the archaeological record. These issues challenge archaeologists to achieve a new a level of precision and insight, because what we are trying to see in archaeological remains is the reflections of people's cultural identity, something that is difficult to identify even in ethnographic settings.

In the centuries before A.D. 600 there was a kind of frontier between the descendants of the relatively recent Saladoid migrants on the east and the people who had been living in the Greater Antilles for thousands of years on the west. The frontier was between Puerto Rico and Hispaniola but also included eastern Hispaniola and probably western Puerto Rico. How fluid was this frontier? How much interaction took place across it and through what channels? As discussed in Chapter 4, the scenario that South American potters and farmers moved into through the Lesser Antilles to Puerto Rico, paused there for over 500 years, and then finally resumed their colonization of the rest of the Caribbean is no longer credible. Cultural interaction and change was certainly taking place across this frontier constantly and is attested to archaeologically by sites such as El Caimito (Chapter 4). The rapid spread of horticulture and pottery use in Hispaniola, Jamaica, Cuba, and the Bahamas is becoming better known, and it is increasingly clear that it reflects changing economic and cultural practices more than it does the mass movement of people. Certainly migrations were involved, especially into Jamaica, Cuba, and the Bahamas but on Hispaniola migrants from Puerto Rico would have joined an already sizable and long-established population. Another way to see it is that after a long period of cultural interaction along the Saladoid–Archaic frontier, there was an explosion of cultural change that affected all of the

Greater Antilles and beyond. Although we can see the effects, including the rapid expansion of population throughout the region, our understanding of how and why these changes came about is not at all refined.

Culture change and population growth are two important trends related to the emergence of larger and larger polities in the Greater Antilles. Another trend that is relevant to these sociopolitical developments is the increasing significance of community activities, as reflected in the creation of ball courts and ceremonial plazas. These constructions became larger and more plentiful on Puerto Rico in the last 500 years before European conquest. On Hispaniola they became even larger. Although initially following the Puerto Rican pattern of multiple courts with variable configurations (as at the site of El Atajadizo in easternmost Dominican Republic), later constructions in the interior were single features and were very much larger than any that had existed before (as at Chacuey or San Juan de la Maguana). This trend parallels the emergence of more powerful *caciques* and of fewer and larger polities – the sort of situation described by European observers on Hispaniola, Cuba, and Puerto Rico after 1492. At the time of conquest these polities still seemed to be increasing in size.

Despite sharing certain characteristics, we should not conclude that the complex Caribbean polities of late prehistory were all the same. In fact, they were different in structure and origin and different in the basis of their centralized authority. As discussed in Chapters 3 and 4, this diversity can be obscured if we use the neo-evolutionary concepts and terminology that were in use in anthropology a generation ago. The sorts of polities that existed in the Greater Antilles might all be seen as "chiefdoms" of some sort or other, but this characterization masks their significant differences, and these differences have not been adequately explored. A polity in the interior valley of Hispaniola might represent the ascendancy of a single lineage that has emerged over many generations, where in Puerto Rico the largest political entities were probably confederacies of groups who were relatively equal in power and prestige, acting in concert for their mutual benefit. On Cuba, in contrast to both of these models, the largest polities may have been relatively short-lived attempts to impose a hegemonic structure from outside of the island, almost as beachhead colonies.

Similar kinds of political centralization were not taking place in the Lesser Antilles in the last centuries before the Europeans' arrival. As discussed in Chapter 5, both the southern and northern Lesser Antilles were in the midst of poorly understood changes involving interactions with forces to the south and west. The southern Windward Islands had extensive contact with the South American mainland, involving trade, intermarriage, and probably population movement. Evidence from the northern Lesser Antilles, from the Virgin Islands to Guadeloupe, suggests that the islands were coming under more direct influence from the Greater Antilles. Between these two groups of islands, a buffer zone may have existed – an area of little settlement or complete depopulation. On the eve of European contact the situation appeared to be in the midst of active change.

In late prehistoric times and after European contact it is apparent that there was a great deal of cultural diversity in the Caribbean. In the most general terms, the archipelago had been colonized and recolonized several times from at least two different mainland areas. There had also been long periods of time that would have allowed for cultural and linguistic divergence. The result was a mosaic of cultural identities, some closely related and some very different. Even on single islands, notably Hispaniola and Cuba, there were several distinct cultural groups.

THEMES AND DIRECTIONS FOR FUTURE RESEARCH

In much of the preceding summary, the shortcomings of our current understanding and the need for new research are apparent. It may seem disappointing to end this volume with a list of things we do not know, but to do so is also to acknowledge that some of the most interesting and exciting issues in the archaeology of the Caribbean are as yet unresolved. They offer the next generation of Caribbean scholars challenges and questions that are as complex and important as those faced by earlier generations.

Here are some of the themes that have come up repeatedly in this volume that seem to be promising directions for future work.

In many cases these topics are already the subject of current research and debate.

One important area for future research involves the cultural variability in the Caribbean that was just mentioned. What were the processes of culture change and ethnogenesis that account for the region's heterogeneity, and how are we to understand the processes of cultural divergence, hybridity, and synthesis that seem to have occurred many times in the Caribbean? What impact did this diversity have on the course of Caribbean history, where so many times period of intense culture contact seem to correspond with periods of dramatic cultural change? These questions demand that archaeologists find better ways to use archaeological data to explore complex issues of cultural identity. Part of this approach may be to improve our understanding the physical relationships between individuals, using DNA or other physical techniques. Another possible approach (already in practice by many) is to pay careful attention to microstylistic variability within artifact classes, particularly ceramics.

Another important area of research involves the archaeology of households and kinship units. For nearly all of Caribbean prehistory, large multigenerational households were the basic unit of production, supplying food and goods for all of its members. Households were also the basic unit of social organization, and so they are a natural focus for many kinds of archaeological questions. Detailed attention to domestic production and food practices also sheds light on cultural identity and change. Research on households and larger social phenomena has required a shift in archaeological methodology. When archaeologists were trying to understand chronological changes in artifact assemblages, stratigraphic excavations in deeply layered trash deposits were an efficient and rewarding way to proceed. Questions of the spatial organization of activities in large households, however, call for larger scale horizontal excavation strategies, exposing whole houses and their associated activity areas.

Understanding prehistoric economies involves developing a richer understanding of prehistoric ecosystems and the patterns of environmental change that took place under human occupation. The impact of the arrival of people and all they brought with them (e.g., dogs and other exotic animals and plants) was considerable, but the dynamics of this change are not well understood. Island settings are proving to be good places to measure the effects of human predation and land use on animal populations and local flora. The relationship between people and the environment should be considered a sensitive indicator of cultural practices as well as economic adaptation.

Many questions of kinship organization, status differentiation, cultural interaction, and political complexity call for research foci at scales even larger than households, including the organization of structures and features in a village and their relationships to one another and the spatial organization of settlements and polities in the landscape. Using this regional-scale data, archaeologists are also tackling questions of regional demographic change and the specialized production and distribution of goods.

Another area of continuing interest, discussed extensively in this volume, involves understanding the emergence and structure of complex polities of later prehistory. As mentioned in previous chapters, there is a great deal we do not know about how and why complex societies developed in the Caribbean. In fact, comparatively little detailed research has been carried out in contexts that would shed light on the earliest stages of this process. We need to continue the work of reconstructing the demography of the Caribbean in the first millennium A.D. This has been done with some success on small islands or in parts of large islands, but the size of the region as a whole is not so vast that we could not imagine reconstructing the paleodemography of the whole archipelago.

At the same time, we need to pay attention to the relationship of demography to technologies of food production. By the time of European conquest, food production in the Greater Antilles was complex and specialized. How were economic changes related to changes in demography? In exploring these material indications of human activity, we can use some of the most refined and robust methodologies in the archaeologists' toolkit. We must also be attentive to the strategies and aims of individuals and families, as they sought to turn the circumstances of their social, political, and economic life to their best advantage. The agency of individuals is reflected in every part of the archaeological record, but it is particularly important to attempt to understand how the symbolism of power and ideology changed through time – how these symbolic systems were purposefully manipulated through the active interventions of the people involved.

A final theme for continued research involves the significant continuity that exists between the Caribbean societies that existed before and after European conquest. It has been easy to imagine a stark divide between the indigenous and the modern Caribbean – between prehistory and history. As noted earlier, there are many aspects of Caribbean culture involving economic practices, foods and the names for foods, and ways of relating to the environment and to other people that show that the cultural interactions and continuity between the indigenous and historic peoples were substantial and continuing. I believe that those creating the written history of the early colonial period, mostly Europeans with some education, either didn't understand the extent and importance of this cultural, linguistic, and biological continuity or minimized its significance in their records. Historical archaeology can allow us to produce a much better understanding of this period, which is so critical to understanding contemporary Caribbean cultures.

The history of the Caribbean is a remarkable story of people adapting to a place that for many is the symbol of paradise – a rich and beautiful archipelago with a glorious climate and abundant resources. In this extraordinary setting, Caribbean history unfolded in unique ways. There were long periods with little noticeable change: dozens of generations in succession lived in the same places and in the same ways that their parents and grandparents lived. There were many periods of cultural interaction, as people with different histories, customs, and languages lived side by side and together evolved new cultures. And there were periods of dramatic cultural change – some of them cataclysmic – as when Europeans conquered the region and set into motion an enormous and lasting migration of people from Europe, Africa, and Asia. As catastrophic as the European's arrival was for the indigenous people of the Caribbean, it should not be seen as the end of one history and the beginning of another. Rather, this episode should be seen as another arrival in a series of arrivals, another transition in a series of transitions, and another chapter in the long, rich, and continuing history that all Caribbean people share.

BIBLIOGRAPHY

Agorsah, Kofi 1995 Vibrations of maroons and marronage in Caribbean history and archaeology. *In* Proceedings of the Fifteenth International Congress for the Study of Pre-Columbian Cultures of the Lesser Antilles. Puerto Rico: I.A.C.A.

Alegría, Ricardo E. 1983 Ball Courts and Ceremonial Plazas in the West Indies. New Haven: Yale University Publications in Anthropology, No. 79.

Allaire, Louis 1990 Prehistoric Taino interaction with the Lesser Antilles: the view from Martinique, F. W. I. 90. Notes: Paper presented at the 55th annual meeting of the Society for American Archaeology, Las Vegas, Nevada, April 18–22, 1990.

Allaire, Louis 1991 Understanding Suazey. *In* Proceedings of the Thirteenth International Congress for the Study of Pre-Columbian Cultures of the Lesser Antilles. Curaçao: Reports of the Archaeological and Anthropological Institute of the Netherlands Antilles, No. 9, pp. 715–728.

Allaire, Louis 1996 Visions of cannibals: Distant islands and distant lands in Taino World Image. *In* The Lesser Antilles in the Age of European Expansion. Robert L. Paquette and Stanley L. Engerman, eds. Pp. 33–49. Gainesville: University Press of Florida.

Allaire, Louis 1997 The Caribs of the Lesser Antilles. *In* The Indigenous People of the Caribbean. Samuel M. Wilson, ed. Pp. 177–185. Gainesville: University Press of Florida.

Anderson-Córdova, Karen 1990 Hispaniola and Puerto Rico: Indian Acculturation and Heterogeneity, 1492–1550. Ph.D. Dissertation. New Haven: Yale University.

Armstrong, Douglas V. 1978 Archaic Shellfish Gatherers of St. Kitts, Leeward Islands: A Case Study in Subsistence and Settlement Patterns. Unpublished master's thesis, University of California at Los Angeles.

Arrom, José J. 1975 Mitologia y artes prehispánicas de las Antillas. Mexico City: Siglo XXI Editores, s.a.

Arrom, José J. 1997 The creation myths of the Taíno. *In* Taíno: Pre-Columbian Art and Culture from the Caribbean. Bercht Fátima, John A. Farmer, and Dicey Taylor, eds. Pp. 68–79. New York: Monacelli.

Atkinson, Lesley-Gail, ed. 2006 The Earliest Inhabitants: The Dynamics of the Jamaican Taíno. Kingston, Jamaica: University of the West Indies Press.

Barlow, Roger 1832 A Brief Summe of Geographie. London: Hakluyt Society.

Basso, Ellen B. 1995 The Last Cannibals: A South American Oral History. Austin: University of Texas Press.

Beard, J. S. 1949 The Natural Vegetation of the Windward and Leeward Islands. Oxford: Clarendon Press.

Benoît, B., and N. Vidal 2001 Essai de Geographie Ameridienne de La Martinique. *In* Proceedings of the Nineteenth International Congress for the Study of Pre-Columbian Cultures of the Lesser Antilles: Aruba.

Bercht, Fátima, John A. Farmer, and Dicey Taylor 1997 Taíno: Pre-Columbian Art and Culture from the Caribbean. New York: Monacelli Press.

Berman, Mary J., and P. Gnivecki 1991 The colonization of the Bahamas archipelago, a view from the Three Dog Site, San Salvador. *In* Proceedings of the Fourteenth International Congress for the Study of Pre-Columbian Cultures of the Lesser Antilles. Barbados: Barbados Museum and Historical Society. Pp. 170–181.

Berman, Mary J., and P. Gnivecki 1995 The Colonization of the Bahama Archipelago: A Reappraisal. World Archaeology 26(3):421–441.

Blanchon, Paul, and John Shaw 1995 Reef drowning during the last deglaciation: Evidence for catastrophic sea-level rise and ice-sheet collapse. Geology 23(1):4–8.

Blume, Helmut 1972 The Caribbean Islands. London: Longman Group Limited.

Bonnissent, Dominique 1995 Les caractéristiques de la ceramique du site de Hope Estate, Ile de Saint Martin. *In* Proceedings of the Sixteenth Congress of the International Association for Caribbean Archaeology. P. 95. Basse Terre, Guadeloupe: Conseil Régional de la Guadeloupe.

Boomert, A. 1986 The Cayo Complex of St. Vincent: Ethnohistorical and archaeological aspects of the Island Carib problem. Antropológica 663–668.

Boomert, Arie 2000 Trinidad, Tobago and the Lower Orinoco Interaction Sphere: An Archaeological/Ethnohistorical Study. Alkmaar: Cairi.

Boomert, Arie, and Peter Harris 1988 An Inventory of the Archaeological Sites in Trinidad and Tobago. Report 3: A Classification in Terms of Cultural Resource Management. St. Augustine, Trinidad: University of the West Indies.

Boromé, Joseph 1966 Spain and Dominica 1493–1647. *Caribbean Quarterly* 12(4):30–46.

Bourne, Edward G. 1906 Ramón Pané: Treatise on the antiquities of the Indians of Haiti, which he as one who knows their language diligently collected by the command of the admiral [Christopher Columbus]. American Antiquarian Society Proceedings 17:318–338.

Boyrie de Moya, Emile de 1955 Monumento Megalitico y Petroglifos de Chacuey, República Dominicana. Ciudad Trujillo, R. D.: Publicacaciones de la Universidad de Santo Domingo, Serie VII, Volumen XCVII, No. 1.

Boyrie de Moya, Emile de 1960 Cinco años de arqueología Dominicana. Revista Anales 26(93–96):23–98.

Braun, Barbara, and Peter G. Roe 1995 Arts of the Amazon. London: Thames and Hudson.

Breton, Raymond 1892 Dictionnaire Caraïbe-François. Leipzig: Jules Platzman.

Brokke, Alex J. 1999 Shell. *In* Archaeological Investigations on St. Martin (Lesser Antilles). Corinne L. Hofman and Menno L. P. Hoogland, eds. Pp. 47–50. Leiden: Faculty of Archaeology, Leiden University.

Broodbank, Cyprian 2000 An Island Archaeology of the Early Cyclades. Cambridge: Cambridge University Press.

Bullen, Ripley P., and F. W. Sleight 1963 The Krum Bay Site: A preceramic site on St. Thomas, United States Virgin Islands. The William L. Bryant Foundation, American Studies Report 5:63.

Burrage, Henry S., ed. 1906 Early English and French Voyages Chiefly from Hakluyt 1534–1608. New York: C. Scribner's Sons.

Calendar of State Papers 1889 Calendar of State Papers, Colonial Series, America and West Indies, 1669–1674. London: Eyre and Spottiswoode.

Callaghan, R. T. 1985 Antillean cultural contacts with mainland regions as a navigation problem. *In* Proceedings of the Fifteenth International Congress for the Study of Pre-Columbian Cultures of the Lesser Antilles. San Juan, Puerto Rico: Centro de Estudios Avanzados de Puerto Rico y el Caribe, pp. 181–190.

Callaghan, Richard T. 2001 Ceramic Age Seafaring and Interaction Potential in the Antilles: A Computer Simulation. Current Anthropology; Volume 42 (2001), pp. 308–313.

Callaghan, R. T., and Donna Fremont 1992 A computer simulation of routes of passage in the Caribbean and Gulf of Mexico. Paper presented at the 57th annual meeting of the Society for American Archaeology, Pittsburgh, Pennsylvania.

Cambridge University Press 1977–2000 The Cambridge History of the Native Peoples of the Americas. Volume 1: North America; Volume 2: Mesoamerica; Volume 3: South America. Cambridge: Cambridge University Press.

Carlson, L. A. 1999 First Contact: The Coralie Site, Grand Turk, Turks and Caicos Islands. Gainesville: University Press of Florida.

Carmine, John, ed. 1997 Material Harm: Archaeological Studies of War and Violence. Glasgow: Cruithne.

Carneiro, Robert L. 1981 The Chiefdom: Precursor of the State. *In* The Transition to Statehood in the New World. G. D. Jones and R. R. Kautz, eds. pp. 37–79. Cambridge and New York: Cambridge University Press.

Cassá, Roberto. 1974 Los Taínos de la Española. Santo Domingo, Dominican Republic: Editora de la Universidad Autónoma de Santo Domingo.

Chanlatte Baik, Luis A. 1976 La Hueca y Sorcé (Vieques, Puerto Rico): Nuevo Esquema para los Procesos Culturales de la Arqueología Antillana. Santo Domingo: Fundación García Arévalo.

Chanlatte Baik, Luis A. 1979 Excavaciones arqueológicas en Vieques. Revista Del Museo Del Antropología, Historia y Arte De La Universidad De Puerto Rico 1:55–9.

Chanlatte Baik, Luis A. 1981 La Hueca y Sorcé (Vieques, Puerto Rico). Primeras Migraciónes Agroalfareras Antillanas: Nuevo Esquema para los Procesos Culturales de la Arqueología Antillana. Santo Domingo.

Chanlatte Baik, Luis A. 1990 Cultura Ostionoide – Un Desarrollo Agroalfarero Antillano. *In* Proceedings of the Eleventh International Congress for the Study of Pre-Columbian Cultures of the Lesser Antilles. San Juan, Puerto Rico: La Fundacion Arqueólogica, Antropológica e Historica de Puerto Rico, pp. 295–310.

Chanlatte Baik, Luis A. 1995 Presencia Huecoide en Hacienda Grande, Loiza, Puerto Rico. *In* Proceedings of the Fifteenth International Congress for the Study of Pre-Columbian Cultures of the Lesser Antilles. San Juan, Puerto Rico: Centro de Estudios Avanzados de Puerto Rico y el Caribe, pp. 501–515.

Chanlatte Baik, Luis A. 2003 Agricultural Societies of the Caribbean: The Greater Antilles and the Bahamas. *In* General History of the Caribbean. Vol I: Autochthonous Societies. Jalil Sued Badillo, ed. Pp. 228–258. Paris: UNESCO.

Chanlatte Baik, Luis A., and Y. M. Narganes Storde 1980 La Hueca Vieques: Nuevo Complejo Cultural Agroalfarero en la Arqueologicia Antillana. *In* Proceedings of the Eighth International Congress for the Study of Pre-Columbian Cultures of the Lesser Antilles. Tempe, Arizona: Arizona State Anthropological Research Papers Number 22, pp. 501–523.

Chanlatte Baik, Luis A. and Y. M. Narganes Storde 2005 *Cultura La Hueca. Río Piedras*, Puerto Rico. Museo de Historia, Antropología y Arte, Universidad de Puerto Rico, Recinto de Río Piedras.

Charlevoix, Pierre Xavier François de 1731–1733 Histoire de l'Isle Espagnole ou de S. Domingue. Paris: Chez François Barois.

Coe, William R. I. 1957 A distinctive artifact common to Haiti and Central America. American Antiquity 22:280–282.

Cook, S. F., and W. Borah 1971 The aboriginal population of Hispaniola. *In* Essays in Population History. Volume 1: Mexico and the Caribbean. Pp. 376–410. Berkeley: University of California Press.

Crock, John G. and James B. Petersen 2004 Inter-island exchange, settlement hierarchy, and a Taino-related chiefdom on the Anguilla Bank, Northern Lesser Antilles. *In* Late ceramic age societies in the Eastern Caribbean. André Delpuech, and Corinne L. Hofman, eds. BAR: Paris Monographs in American Archaeology 14: pp. 139–58.

Crock, John G., James B. Petersen, and Nik Douglas 1995 Preceramic Anguilla: A view from the Whitehead's Bluff site. *In* Proceedings of the Fifteenth

International Congress for the Study of Pre-Columbian Cultures of the Lesser Antilles. Pp. 283–292.

Crosby, Alfred W. 1975 The Columbian Exchange: Biological and Cultural Consequences of 1492. Westport, CT: Greenwood Pub. Co.

Cruxent, José M., and Irving Rouse 1982 Arqueología Cronologica de Venezuela. Caracas, Venezuela: Ernesto Armitano.

Cruxent, José M., and Irving Rouse 1969 Early man in the West Indies. Scientific American 221(5):42–52.

Cunningham, Richard L. 1997 The biological impacts of 1492. *In* The Indigenous People of the Caribbean. Samuel M. Wilson, ed. Pp. 29–35. Gainesville: University of Florida Press.

Curet, Luis A. 1997 Technological changes in prehistoric ceramics from eastern Puerto Rico: An exploratory study. Journal of Archaeological Science 24:497–504.

Curet, Luis A. 2003 Issues on the diversity and emergence of middle-range societies of the ancient Caribbean: A critique. Journal of Archaeological Research 11(1):1–42.

Curet, Luis A. 2005 Caribbean Paleodemography: Population, Culture History, and Sociopolitical Processes in Ancient Puerto Rico. Tuscaloosa: University of Alabama Press.

Curet, Luis A., and José R. Oliver 1998 Mortuary practices, social development, and ideology in precolumbian Puerto Rico. Latin American Antiquity 9(3):217–239.

Curet, Luis A., and Luis A. Rodríguez Gracia 1995 Informe preliminar del proyecto arqueológico de Tibes. *In* Proceedings of the Fourteenth International Congress for the Study of Pre-Columbian Cultures of the Lesser Antilles. Vol. 1, pp. 113–126.

Davis, Dave D. 1974 Some notes concerning the Archaic occupation of Antigua. *In* Proceedings of the Fifth International Congress for the Study of Pre-Columbian clutures of the Lesser Antilles. Pp. 65–71, 74.

Davis, Dave D. 1993 Archaic blade production on Antigua, West Indies. American Antiquity 58(4):688–697.

Davis, Dave D. 2000 Jolly Beach and the Preceramic Occupation of Antigua, West Indies. New Haven: Yale University Publications in Anthropology.

Deagan, Kathleen 1995 Puerto Real: The Archaeology of a Sixteenth-Century Spanish Town in Hispaniola. Gainesville: University Press of Florida.

Deagan, Kathleen A. 2004 Reconsidering Taíno Social Dynamics after Conquest: Gender and Class in Culture contact Studies. American Antiquity 69(4):597–626.

de Booy, Theodoor 1919 Archaeology of the Virgin Islands. Museum of the American Indian, Heye Foundation, Indian Notes and Monographs 1(1):19.

DeBoer, Warren R. 1981 Buffer zones in the cultural ecology of aboriginal Amazonia: An ethnohistorical approach. American Antiquity 46:364–377.

Delpuech, André, and Corinne L. Hofman 2004 Late Ceramic Age Societies in the Eastern Caribbean. Oxford: BAR International Series.

Delpuech, André, Corinne L. Hofman, and Menno Hoogland. 2003 Amerindian Settlements & Archaeological Reality in the Lesser Antilles: Case of Grande-Terre, Guadeloupe. *In* Proceedings of the Nineteenth International Congress for the Study of Pre-Columbian Cultures of the Lesser Antilles.

DeWolf, Marian 1953 Excavations in Jamaica. American Antiquity 18(3):230–238.

Diamond, Jared M. 1999 Guns, Germs, and Steel: The Fates of Human Societies. New York: W. W. Norton.

Digerfeldt, G., and M. D. Hendry 1987 An 8000-year Holocene sea-level record from Jamaica: Implications for interpretation of Caribbean reef and coastal history. Coral Reefs 5(4):165–169.

Dobyns, Henry F. 1976 Native American Historical Demography. Bloomington: University of Indiana Press.

Dobyns, Henry F. 1983 Their Number Become Thinned: Native American Population Dynamics in Eastern North America. Knoxville: University of Tennessee Press.

Donovan S. K., and Trevor A. Jackson 1994 Caribbean Geology: An Introduction. Kingston, Jamaica: University of the West Indies Publishers' Association.

Drennan, R. D., and C. A. Uribe, eds. 1987 Chiefdoms in the Americas. Lanham, Md.: University Press of America.

Du Tertre, Jean B. 1667 Histoire Générale des Antilles Habitées par les Français. Paris: Jolly.

Dunn, Oliver, and James E. Kelley, Jr. 1989 The Diario of Christopher Columbus's First Voyage to America 1492–1493. Norman: University of Oklahoma Press.

Durand, J., and Henry Petitjean Roget 1991 A propos d'un collier funeraire a Morel, Guadeloupe: Les Huecoide sont-ils un mythe? *In* Proceedings of the Twelfth International Congress for the Study of Pre-Columbian Cultures of the Lesser Antilles: French Guiana. Pp. 53–72.

Earle, Timothy 1991 Chiefdoms: Power, Economy, and Ideology. New York and Cambridge: Cambridge University Press.

Ekholm, Gordon 1961 Puerto Rican stone collars as ballgame belts. *In* Essays in Pre-Columbian Art and Archaeology. Vol. 61. Cambridge, Mass.: Harvard University Press. Pp. 356–71.

Evans, Clifford, and Betty J. Meggers 1960 Archaeological investigations in British Guiana. Washington, DC: Smithsonian Institution, Bureau of American Ethnology Bulletin 177.

Febles Dueñas, Jorge 1995 Taíno: Arqueología de Cuba, Havana: Centro de Antropología, CEDISAC (CD-ROM).

Feinman, G., and J. Neitzel 1984 Too many types: An overview of sedentary prestate societies in the Americas. Advances in Archaeological Method and Theory 7:39–102.

Fewkes, Jesse W. 1907 The aborigines of Porto Rico and neighboring islands. Bureau of American Ethnology Annual Report 25:1–220.

Fewkes, Jesse W. 1922 A prehistoric island cluture area of America. Bureau of American Ethnology Annual Report 34:22.

Figueredo, Alfredo E. 1974 History of Virgin Islands archeology. Journal of the Virgin Islands Archaeological Society 1:1–6.

Figueredo, Alfredo E. 1976 Caño Hondo, un residuario preceramico en la isla de Vieques. *In* Proceedings of the Sixth International Congress for the Study of Pre-Columbian Cultures of the Lesser Antilles. Pp. 247–252.

Floyd, Troy S. 1973 The Columbus Dynasty in the Caribbean, 1492–1526. Albuquerque: University of New Mexico Press.

Forte, Janette 1996 About Guyanese Amerindians. Georgetown, Guyana: J. Forte.

García Goyco, Osvaldo, Adalberto Maurás, Edwin Crespo, and Jeff Walker 1995 Paso del Indio Archaeological Site, Vega Baja, Puerto Rico. Handout accompanying poster session, presented July 24–29 at the 16th International Congress for Caribbean Archaeology. P. 95.

Gonzalez, Nancie L. 1988 Sojourners of the Caribbean. Urbana: University of Illinois Press.

González Colón, Juan 1984 Tibes: Un centro ceremonial indígena. Master's thesis, Centro de Estudios Avanzados de Puerto Rico y el Caribe.

Goodwin, R. C. 1978a The history and development of osteology in the Caribbean area. Revista Interamericana 8(3):463–494.

Goodwin, R. C. 1978b The Lesser Antillean archaic: New data from St. Kitts. Journal of the Virgin Islands Archaeological Society 5:6–16.

Granberry, Julian 1991 Was Ciguayo a West Indian Hokan language? International Journal of American Linguistics 57(4):514–520.

Granberry, Julian, and Gary S. Vescelius 2004 Languages of the Pre-Columbian Antilles. Tuscaloosa: University of Alabama Press.

Guarch Delmonte, José 1972 Excavaciones en el extremo oriental de Cuba. Havana: Academia de Ciencias de Cuba, Serie Arqueológica, No. 1.

Hakluyt, Richard 1904 The Principal Navigations Voyages Traffiques and Discoveries of the English Nation, Volume X. Glasgow: Hakluyt Society.

Harrington, M. R. 1921 Cuba Before Columbus (2 vols.). New York: Museum of the American Indian, Heye Foundation.

Harris, Peter 1972 Notes on Trinidad Archaeology. Pointe-a-Pierre: Trinidad and Tobago Historical Society.

Harris, Peter 1973 Preliminary report on Banwari Trace, a preceramic site in Trinidad. *In* Proceedings of the Fourth International Congress for the Study of Pre-Columbian Cultures of the Lesser Antilles. Pp. 115–125.

Harris, Peter 1976 The preceramic period in Trinidad. *In* Proceedings of the First Puerto Rican Symposium of Archaeology. L. S. Robinson, ed. Pp. 33–65. Puerto Rico: Santurce.

Harris, Peter 1978 A revised chronological framework for Ceramic Trinidad and Tobago. *In* Proceedings of the Seventh International Congress for the Study of Pre-Columbian Cultures of the Lesser Antilles: Caracas, Venezuela. Pp. 47–63.

Hatt, Gudmund 1924 Archaeology of the Virgin Islands. *In* Proceedings of the 21st International Congress of Americanists. Vol. 1, pp. 29–42.

Haviser, Jay B. 1999 Lithics. *In* Archaeological Investigations on St. Martin (Lesser Antilles). Corinne L. Hofman and Menno L. P. Hoogland, eds. Pp. 189–213. Leiden, Netherlands: Faculty of Archaeology, Leiden University.

Heckenberger, Michael J. 2002 Rethinking the Arawakan diaspora: Hierarchy, regionality, and the Amazonian Formative. *In* Comparative Arawakan Histories: Rethinking Language Family and Culture Area in Amazonia. Jonathan D. Hill and Fernando Santos-Granero, eds. Pp. 99–122. Urbana: University of Illinois Press.

Heckenberger, Michael, James B. Petersen, and E. G. Neves 1999 Village size and permanance in Amazonia: two archaeological examples from Brazil. Latin American Antiquity 10(4):353–76.

Helms, Mary 1979 Ancient Panama: Chiefs in Search of Power. Austin: University of Texas Press.

Helms, Mary 1988 Ulysses' Sail: An Ethnographic Odyssey of Power, Knowledge, and Geographical Distance. Princeton: Princeton University Press.

Henige, David 1978 On the contact population of Hispaniola: History as higher mathematics. Hispanic American Historical Review 58:217–237.

Henocq, Christophe, and François Petit 1995 Presentation de six sites arqueologiques de Saint-Martin et de leur environnement. In Proceedings of the Sixteenth International Congress for the Study of Pre-Columbian Cultures of the Lesser Antilles: Guadeloupe. Vol. 1, pp. 300–315.

Herrera, Antonio de 1975 Historia General de las Indias. Translated as Historia de la Conquista de la Isla Española de Santo Domingo by Luis Joseph Peguero in 1762. Santo Domingo: Museo de Las Casas Reales.

Hester, T. R., H. J. Shafer, and J. D. Eaton 1994 Continuing Archaeology at Colha, Belize. Austin: Texas Archeological Research Lab.

Highfield, Arnold R. 1997 Some observations on the Taino language. *In* The Indigenous People of the Caribbean. Samuel M. Wilson, ed. Pp. 154–168. Gainesville: University Press of Florida.

Hodder, Ian, and C. Orton 1976 Spatial Analysis in Archaeology. New York and Cambridge: Cambridge University Press.

Hofman, Corinne L. 1993 In Search of the Native Population of Pre-Columbian Saba (400–1450 A.D.). Part One: Pottery Styles and Their Interpretations. Leiden: Rijksuniversiteit te Leiden.

Hofman, Corinne L. 1999 Pottery. *In* Archaeological Investigations on St. Martin (Lesser Antilles). Corinne L. Hofman and Menno L. P. Hoogland, eds. Pp. 149–187. Leiden, Netherlands: Faculty of Archaeology, Leiden University.

Hofman, Corinne L., Menno Hoogland, and André Delpuech 2001 Spatial organisation at a Troumassoid settlement: The case of Anse La Gourde, Guadeloupe. *In* Proceedings of the Nineteenth International Congress for the Study of Pre-Columbian Cultures of the Lesser Antilles: Aruba, Vol I: 124–41.

Hofman, Corinne L., and Menno L. P. Hoogland 1999 Archaeological Investigations on St. Martin (Lesser Antilles). Leiden, Netherlands: Faculty of Archaeology, Leiden University.

Hofman, Corinne L., and Menno L. P. Hoogland 2004. Social dynamics and change in the Northern Lesser Antilles. *In* Late Ceramic Age Societies in the Eastern Caribbean, André Delpuech and Corinne L. Hofman, eds. BAR: Paris Monographs in American Archaeology 14: pp. 47–58.

Hoogland, Menno L. P. 1999 Methods and strategies. *In* Archaeological Investigations on St. Martin (Lesser Antilles). Corinne L. Hofman and Menno L. P. Hoogland, eds. Pp. 129–147. Leiden, Netherlands: Faculty of Archaeology, Leiden University.

Hulme, Peter 1986 Colonial Encounters: Europe and the Native Caribbean, 1492–1797. London: Methuen & Co.

Hulme, Peter, and Neil L. Whitehead 1992 Wild Majesty: Encounters with Caribs from Columbus to the Present Day. Oxford: Clarendon Press.

Jane, Cecil 1988 The Voyage of Christopher Columbus. London: Argonaut Press.

Jefferson, Thomas 1801 Notes on the State of Virginia. Newark, N.J.: Pennyington & Gould.

Jones, John G. 1994 Pollen evidence for early settlement and agriculture in northern Belize. Palynology 18:205–211.

Kapchan, Deborah A., and Pauline T. Strong 1999 Introduction: Theorizing the hybrid. Journal of American Folklore 112(445):1–15.

Keegan, William F. 1987 Diffusion of Maize from South America: The Antillean Connection Reconstructed. *In* Emergent Horticultural Economies of the Eastern Woodlands, W. F. Keegan, ed. Center for Archaeological Investigations Occasional Paper 7, pp. 329–344. Southern Illinois University, Carbondale.

Keegan, William F. 1989 Creating the Guanahatabey (Ciboney): The modern genesis of an extinct culture. Antiquity 63(239):373–379.

Keegan, William F. 1992 The People Who Discovered Columbus: The Prehistory of the Bahamas. Gainesville: University Press of Florida.

Keegan, William F. 1996 Columbus was a cannibal: Myth and the first encounters. *In* The Lesser Antilles in the Age of European Expansion. Robert L. Paquette and Stanley L. Engerman, eds. Pp. 17–32. Gainesville: University Press of Florida.

Keegan, William F. 1997a No man [or woman] is an island: elements of Taino social organization. In Samuel M. Wilson, ed., The Indigenous People of the Caribbean, pp. 109–116. Gainesville: University Press of Florida.

Keegan, William F. 1997b Bahamian Archaeology: Life in the Bahamas and Turks and Caicos before Columbus. Nassau: Media Publishing.

Keegan, William F. 2000 West Indian archaeology. Volume 3: Ceramic age. Journal of Archaeological Research 8:135–167.

Keegan, William F. 2006 Archaic influences in the origins and development of Taino societies. Caribbean Journal of Science 42(1):1–10.

Keegan, William F. n.d. Archaic influences in the origins and development of Taino societies. Unpublished manuscript.

Keegan, William F., Corinne L. Hofman, and Menno Hoogland 2002 An archaeological reconnaissance of St. Lucia. Annual Report of the Museum of Natural History, Gainesville, Florida.

Keegan, William F., M. Maclachlan, and B. Byrne 1998 Social foundations of Taino caciques. *In* Chiefdoms and Chieftaincy in the Americas. E. M. Redmond, ed. Gainesville: University Press of Florida.

Keegan, William F., and Reniel Rodríguez Ramos 2005 Sin Rodeo. El Caribe Arqueológico 8:8–13.

Kerchache, Jacques 1994 L'Arte Taïno. Paris: Musée du Petit Palais.

Kirch, Patrick V. 1984 The Evolution of the Polynesian Chiefdoms. New York and Cambridge: Cambridge University Press.

Kirch, Patrick V. 1997 The Lapita People: Ancestors of the Oceanic World. Cambridge, Mass.: Blackwell.

Knippenberg, Sebastiaan 1999a Lithics. *In* Archaeological Investigations on St. Martin (Lesser Antilles). Corinne L. Hofman and Menno L. P. Hoogland, eds. Pp. 35–46. Leiden: Faculty of Archaeology, Leiden University.

Knippenberg, Sebastiaan 1999b Methods and strategies. *In* Archaeological Investigations on St. Martin (Lesser Antilles). Corinne L. Hofman and Menno L. P. Hoogland, eds. Pp. 25–34. Leiden: Faculty of Archaeology, Leiden University.

Koslowski, Janusz K. 1974 Perceramic Cultures in the Caribbean. Krakow: Panstwowe Wydawn. Naukowe, Oddz. w Krakowie.

Labat, P. J.-B. 1642 Nouveau Voyage aux Iles d'Amérique. Paris: Theodore Legras.

Lambert, Patricia M., ed. 2000 Bioarchaeological Studies of Life in the Age of Agriculture a View from the Southeast. Tuscaloosa: University of Alabama Press.

Las Casas, Frey Bartolomé de 1951 Historia de las Indias (3 vols.). Mexico City: Fondo de Cultura Económica.

Las Casas, Frey Bartolomé de 1967 Apologética Historia Summaria (3 vols.). Mexico City: Universidad Nacional Autónoma de México, Instituto de Investigaciones Históricas.

Lathrap, Donald 1970 The Upper Amazon. New York: Praeger.

Lee, James 1980 Jamaican Redware. *In* Proceedings of the Eighth International Congress for the Study of Pre-Columbian Cultures of the Lesser Antilles. Tempe, Arizona: Arizona State Anthropological Research Papers Number 22, pp. 597–609.

LeRoy Ladurie, Emmanuel. 1981 The Mind and Method of the Historian. Chicago: University of Chicago Press. Translated by Siân and Ben Reynolds.

Loven, Sven 1935 The Origins of Tainan Culture, West Indies. Goteborg: Elanders Bokfryekeri Akfiebolag.

Luna Calderon, Fernando 1976 Preliminary report on the Indian cemetary "El Atajadizo," Dominican Republic. *In* Proceedings of the Sixth International

Congress for the Study of Pre-Columbian Cultures of the Lesser Antilles, Guadeloupe. Pp. 295–303.

Lundberg, Emily R. 1980 Old and new problems in the study of Antillean aceramic traditions. *In* Proceedings of the Eighth International Congress for the Study of Pre-Columbian Cultures of the Lesser Antilles. Tempe, Arizona: Arizona State Anthropological Research Papers Number 22, pp. 131–138.

Lundberg Emily R. 1989 Preceramic Procurement Patterns at Krum Bay, Virgin Islands. PhD Dissertation, University of Illinois, Urbana.

Lundberg, Emily R. 1991 Interrelationships among preceramic complexes of Puerto Rico and the Virgin Islands. *In* Proceedings of the Thirteenth International Congress for the Study of Pre-Columbian Cultures of the Lesser Antilles. Pp. 73–85.

MacArthur, R. H., and E. O. Wilson 1967 The Theory of Island Biogeography. Princeton: Princeton University Press.

MacNeish, Richard S., and Antoinette Nelken-Turner 1983 Final Report of the Belize Archaic Archaeological Reconnaissance. Boston: Center for Archaeological Studies, Boston University.

MacPhee, R. D. E., Jennifer L. White, and Charles A. Woods 2000 New Megalonychid sloths (Phyllophaga, Xenarthra) from the Quaternary of Hispaniola. American Museum Novitates 303:31–32.

Marichal, Pragmacio 1989 Destruccion del monumento indigena de Chacuey. Boletín del Museo del Hombre Dominicano 22:95–105.

Martyr D'Anghera, Peter 1970 De Orbe Novo: The Eight Decades of Peter Martyr D'Anghera. New York: Burt Franklin. Notes: Francis Augustus MacNutt, Trans.

Mason, J. A. 1941 A large archaeological site at Capá, Utuado, with notes on other Porto Rico sites visited in 1914–1915: Scientific Survey of Porto Rico and the Virgin Islands. New York Academy of Sciences Volume 18, part 2.

McGinnis, Shirley A. M. 1997 Ideographic expression in the Precolumbian Caribbean. Austin: University of Texas.

Meggers, Betty J. 1987 Oscilación climática y cronológia cultural en el Caribe. Actas del Tercer Simposio de la Fundación de Arqueología del Caribe. Pp. 23–54. Washington, D.C.: La Fundación de Arqueología del Caribe.

Meggers, Betty J. 1991 Cultural evolution in Amazonia. *In* Profiles in Cultural Evolution. A. T. Rambo and K. Gillogly, eds. Pp. 191–216. Ann Arbor: University of Michigan Museum of Anthropology, Anthropology Papers, No. 85.

Meggers, Betty J., and Clifford Evans 1961 An experimental formulation of horizon styles in the tropical forest area of South America. *In* Essays in Pre-Columbian Art and Archaeology. Pp. 46–82. Cambridge, Mass.: Harvard University Press.

Meggers, Betty J., and Clifford Evans 1978 Lowland South America and the Antilles. *In* Ancient Native Americans. J. D. Jennings, ed. Pp. 543–591. San Francisco: Freeman.

Morse, Birgit F. 1995 The sequence of occupations at the Salt River Site, St Croix, U.S.V.I. *In* Proceedings of the Fifteenth International Congress for the Study of Pre-Columbian Cultures of the Lesser Antilles. San Juan, Puerto Rico: Centro de Estudios Avanzados de Puerto Rico y el Caribe, pp. 495–503.

Moya Pons, Frank 1983 Manual de Historia Dominicana, 7th Ed. Santiago, República Dominica: Universidad Católica Madre y Maestra.

Narganes Storde, Y. M. 1991 Secuencia cronologica de dos sitios arqueologicos de Puerto Rico (Sorce,Vieques y Tecla). *In* Proceedings of the Thirteenth International Congress for the Study of Pre-Columbian Cultures of the Lesser Antilles. Curaçao: Reports of the Archaeological and Anthropological Institute of the Netherlands Antilles, No. 9, pp. 628–646.

Nau, Emile 1894 *Histoire des Caciques d'Haiti*. Paris: Gustave Guérin (also published as Nau, Emilio 1983 *Historia de los Caciques de Haití*. Santo Domingo: Sociedad Dominicana de Bibliófilos, Inc.).

Newsom, Lee A. 1993 Native West Indian Plant Use. Ph.D. Dissertation. Gainesville: University of Florida.

Newsom, Lee A., and Elizabeth S. Wing 2004 On land and sea: Native American uses of biological resources in the West Indies. Tuscaloosa: University of Alabama Press.

Nicholson, Desmond V. 1976 An Antigua shell midden with ceramic and archaic components. *In* Proceedings of the Sixth International Congress for the Study of Pre-Columbian Cultures of the Lesser Antilles. Pointe-a-Pitre, Guadeloupe, pp. 258–263.

Nicholson, Desmond V. 1992 The Archaeology of Antigua and Barbuda. St. John's, Antigua: Museum of Antigua and Barbuda.

Nicholson, Desmond V. 1994 The Archaeology of Antigua and Barbuda. St. Johns, Antigua: Museum of Antigua and Barbuda.

Nokkert, Mark 1999 Faunal exploitation. *In* Archaeological Investigations on St. Martin (Lesser Antilles). Corinne L. Hofman and Menno L. P. Hoogland, eds. Pp. 51–60. Leiden: Faculty of Archaeology, Leiden University.

Nokkert, Mark, Alex J. Brokke, Sebastiaan Knippenberg, and Tom D. Hamburg 1995 An Archaic occupation at Norman Estate, St. Martin. *In* Proceedings of the Sixteenth International Congress for the Study of Pre-Columbian Cultures of the Lesser Antilles, Basse-Terre, Guadeloupe. Pp. 333–351.

Nuñez Jimenez, A. 1948 Mayarí, Descripción General. La Habana: Sociedad Espeleológical de Cuba.

Oliver, José R. 1989 The Archaeological, Linguistic and Ethnohistorical Evidence for the Expansion of Arawakan into Northwestern Venezuela and Northeastern Colombia. Ph.D. Dissertation, Urbana: University of Illinois.

Oliver, José R. 1998 El Centro Ceremonial de Caguana, Puerto Rico: Simbolismo, Iconográfico, Cosmovisión y el Poderío Caciquil Taíno de Borínquen. Oxford: BAR International Series, No. 727.

Oliver, José R. 2005 The Proto-Taíno monumental Cemís of Caguana: A political-religious 'manifesto'. *In* The Archaeology of Puerto Rico. Peter E. Siegel, ed. Tuscaloosa: University of Alabama Press, pp. 230–84.

Orent, Wendy 2004 Plague: The Mysterious Past and Terrifying Future of the World's Most Dangerous Disease. New York: Free Press.

Ortega, Elpidio, and José G. Guerrero 1985 El complejo lítico de la cordillera, las grandes puntas especializadas y su relación con los modos de vida preagroalfareros en la prehistoria de Santo Domingo. *In* Proceedings of the Tenth International Congress for the Study of Pre-Columbian Cultures of the Lesser Antilles. Montreal: Centre de Recherches Caraïbes, pp. 311–334.

Ortega, Elpidio, Marcio Veloz Maggiolo, and Plinio Pina Peña 1976 El Caimito: Un Antiguo complejo ceramista de las Antillas Mayores. *In* Proceedings of the Sixth International Congress for the Study of Pre-Columbian Cultures of the Lesser Antilles, Pointe á Pitre, Guadeloupe. Pp. 276–282.

Oviedo y Valdés, Gonzalo F., de 1959 Historia General y Natural de las Indias (5 vols.). Madrid: Biblioteca de Autores Españoles (Vols. 117–121), Gráficas Orbe.

Pantel, A. G. 1988 Precolumbian Flaked Stone Assemblages in the West Indies. Ph.D. Dissertation. Knoxville: University of Tennessee.

Pané, Ramón 1974 Relación Acerca de las Antigüedades de los Indios. Mexico City: Universidad de México.

Peguero Guzmán, Luis A. 2001 Las plazas ceremoniales como espacio ritual de las culturas Prehistóricas del Caribe: Sus posible vinculaciónes culturales. Boletín del Museo del Hombre Dominicano 29:29–62.

Petersen, James B. 1995 Preliminary analysis of Amerindian ceramics from at Trants, Montserrat. *In* Proceedings of the Fifteenth International Congress for the Study of Pre-Columbian Cultures of the Lesser Antilles. San Juan, Puerto Rico: Centro de Estudios Avanzados de Puerto Rico y el Caribe. Pp.131–141.

Petersen, James B. 1997 Taino, Island Carib, and prehistoric Amerindian economies in the West Indies: tropical forest adaptations to island environments. In Samuel M. Wilson, ed., The Indigenous People of the Caribbean, pp. 118–30. Gainesville: University Press of Florida.

Petersen, James B., Robert N. Bartone, and David R. Watters 1995 Pyroclastic, storm surge, and saladoid villager deposits: The archaeological and geological stratigraphy of the Trants site, Montserrat. *In* Proceedings of the Sixteenth Congress of the International Association for Caribbean Archaeology. Pp. 40–51. Basse Terre: Conseil Régional de la Guadeloupe.

Petersen, James B., and David R. Watters 1991 Archaeological testing at the early Saladoid Trants site, Montserrat, West Indies. *In* Proceedings of the Fourteenth International Congress for the Study of Pre-Columbian Cultures of the Lesser Antilles. Pp. 286–305. Barbados.

Piperno, D., and D. Pearsall 1998 The Origins of Agriculture in the Lowland Neotropics. San Diego: Academic Press.

Purchas, Samuel 1905 Hakluytus Posthumus, or Purchas his Pilgrimes: contayning a history of the world in sea voyages and lande travells by Englishmen and others. Glasgow: J. MacLehose and Sons.

Rainey, F. G. 1941 Excavations in the Ft. Liberté region, Haiti. New Haven: Yale University Publications in Anthropology, No. 23.

Ramenofsky, Ann F. 1987 Vectors of Death: The Archaeology of European Contact. Albuquerque: University of New Mexico Press.

Rand McNally World Atlas 2004. Chicago, IL: Rand McNally & Company.

Ravenstein, E. G. 1908 Martin Behaim: His Life and Globe. London: George Philip & Son, Ltd.

Renfrew, Colin, and John F. Cherry 1986 Peer Polity Interaction and Sociopolitical Change. New York and Cambridge: University of Cambridge Press.

Renfrew, Colin, and Malcolm Wagstaff 1982 An Island Polity: The Archaeology of Exploitation in Melos. New York and Cambridge: Cambridge University Press.

Rey Betancourt, Estrella 1988 Esbozo etnohistórico del siglo XVI temprano en Cuba. Revista Cubana de Ciencias Sociales 16:162–185.

Richardson, Bonham C. 1992 The Caribbean in the Wider World, 1492–1992. New York and Cambridge: Cambridge University Press.

Righter, Elizabeth, and Emily Lundberg 1991 Preliminary report on a prehistoric settlement at Tutu, St. Thomas, U.S. Virgin Islands. *In* Proceedings of the Fourteenth Congress of the International Association for Caribbean Archaeology, pp. 561–576. Barbados: Barbados Museum and Historical Society.

Rodríguez, Miguel 1997 Religious beliefs of the Saladoid people. *In* The Indigenous People of the Caribbean. Samuel M. Wilson, ed. Pp. 80–87. Gainesville: University Press of Florida.

Rodríguez, Miguel 1989 The zoned incised crosshatch (ZIC) ware of early pre-Columbian Ceramic Age sites in Puerto Rico and Vieques Island. *In* Early Ceramic Population Lifeways and Adaptive Strategies in the Caribbean. Peter E. Siegel, ed. Pp. 249–266. Oxford: B.A.R. International Series, No. 506.

Rodríguez, Miguel 1997 Religious beliefs of the Saladoid people. *In* The Indigenous People of the Caribbean. Samuel M. Wilson, ed. Pp. 80–87. Gainesville: University Press of Florida.

Rodríguez, Miguel 1999 Excavaciones en 'Maruca', una Comunidad Arcaica del sur de Puerto Rico. *In* Proceedings of the Seventeenth International Congress for the Study of the Pre-Columbian Cultures of the Lesser Antilles. Rockville Centre, Molloy College. Pp. 166–180.

Rodríguez Ramos, Reniel 2001 Lithic reduction trajectories at La Hueca and Punta Candelero sites, Puerto Rico. Masters Thesis. College Station: Texas A&M University.

Rodríguez Ramos, Reniel 2005 The crab-shell dichotomy revisited: The lithics speak out. *In* Ancient Borinquen: Archaeology and Ethnohistory of Native Puerto Rico. Peter E. Siegel, ed. Tuscaloosa: University of Alabama Press.

Roe, Peter G. 1982 The Cosmic Zygote: Cosmology in the Amazon Basin. New Brunswick, New Jersey: Rutgers University Press.

Roe, Peter G. 1993 Cross Media Isomorphisms in Taino Ceramics and Petroglyphs from Puerto Rico. *In* Proceedings of the Fourteenth International Congress for the Study of Pre-Columbian Cultures of the Lesser

Antilles. Bridgetown, Barbados: Barbados Museum and Historical Society. Pp. 637–655.

Roe, Peter G. 2005 Rivers of stone, rivers within stone: Rock art in Ancient Puerto Rico. *In* Prehistory of Puerto Rico. Peter E. Siegel, ed. Tuscaloosa: University of Alabama Press.

Rogozinski, Jan 2000 A Brief History of the Caribbean: From the Arawak and Carib to the Present. New York: Plume.

Roosevelt, Anna C. 1997 The excavations at Corozal, Venezuela: Stratigraphy and ceramic seriation. New Haven: Yale University Publications in Anthropology, No. 83.

Roumaine, Jacques 1912 L'outillage lithique des Ciboney d'Haiti. Bulletin du Bureau d'Ethnologie de la République d'Haïti 2:22–7.

Rouse, Irving 1939 Prehistory in Haiti: A Study in Method. New Haven: Yale University Publications in Anthropology, No. 21.

Rouse, Irving 1941a An Analysis of the Artifacts of the 1914–1915 Porto Rican Survey: Scientific Survey of Porto Rico and the Virgin Islands. New York Academy of Sciences 18(2):272–295.

Rouse, Irving 1941b Culture of the Ft. Liberté Region, Haiti. New Haven: Yale University Publications in Anthropology, No. 24.

Rouse, Irving 1942 Archaeology of the Maniabon Hills, Cuba. New Haven: Yale University Publications in Anthropology, No. 26.

Rouse, Irving 1952 Porto Rican Prehistory: Scientific Survey of Porto Rico and the Virgin Islands. New York Academy of Sciences 18(3&4).

Rouse, Irving 1964 Prehistory of the West Indies. Science 144(3618):369–375.

Rouse, Irving 1986 Migrations in Prehistory. New Haven: Yale University Press.

Rouse, Irving 1991 Ancestries of the Tainos: Amazonian or Circum-Caribbean. *In* Proceedings of the Thirteenth International Congress for the Study of Pre-Columbian Cultures of the Lesser Antilles. Curaçao: Reports of the Archaeological and Anthropological Institute of the Netherlands Antilles, No. 9. Pp. 682–702.

Rouse, Irving 1992 The Tainos: Rise and Decline of the People Who Greeted Columbus. New Haven: Yale University Press.

Rouse, Irving, and Ricardo E. Alegría 1990 Excavations at María de la Cruz and Hacienda Grande, Loiza, Puerto. New Haven: Yale University Publications in Anthropology, No. 80.

Rouse, Irving, and Louis Allaire 1978 Caribbean Chronology: Chronologies in New World Archaeology. Pp. 431–481. New York: Academic Press.

Rouse, Irving, and José M. Cruxent 1963 Venezuelan Archaeology. New Haven: Yale University Press.

Sahlins, Marshall 1968 Tribesmen. Englewood Cliffs, NJ: Prentice Hall.

Sanoja Obediente, Mario 1980 Los recolectores tempranos del Golfo de Paria, Estado Sucre, Venezuela. *In* Proceedings of the Eighth International Congress for the Study of Pre-Columbian Cultures of the Lesser Antilles. Tempe, Arizona: Arizona State Anthropological Research Papers Number 22, pp. 139–151.

Sanoja Obediente, Mario. 1983 El origen de la sociedad Taína y el Formativo Suramericano. La Cultura Taína. Pp. 37–47. Madrid: Comision Nacional para la Celebracion del V Centenario del Descubrimiento de America.

Sanoja Obediente, Mario, and Iraida Vargas 1978 Antiguas Formaciones y Modos de Producción Venezolanos. Caracas, Venezuela: Monte Avila Editores.

Sanoja Obediente, Mario, and Iraida Vargas 1983 New light on the prehistory of Eastern Venezuela. Advances in New World Archaeology, 2:205–243.

Sauer, Carl O. 1966 The Early Spanish Main. Berkeley: University of California Press.

Schomburgk, Sir R. 1851 Ethnological researches in Santo Domingo. The Athenaeum 1236:719–720.

Siegel, Peter E., ed. 1989a Early Ceramic Population Lifeways and Adaptive Strategies in the Caribbean. Oxford: BAR International Series, No. 506.

Siegel, Peter E. 1989b Site structure, demography, and social complexity in the early Ceramic Age of the Caribbean. *In* Early Ceramic Population Lifeways and Adaptive Strategies in the Caribbean. Peter E. Siegel, ed. Pp. 193–245. Oxford: BAR International Series, No. 506.

Siegel, Peter E. 1992 Ideology, Power, and Social Complexity in Prehistoric Puerto Rico. Ph.D. Dissertation. Binghamton: State University of New York.

Siegel, Peter E. 2004. "What happened after AD 600 in Puerto Rico? Corporate groups, population restructuring, and post-Saladoid social changes. *In* André Delpuech and Corinne L. Hofman, eds., Late Ceramic Age Societies in the Eastern Caribbean. BAR: Paris Monographs in American Archaeology, No. 14, pp. 87–100.

Southey, Thomas. 1827 A Chronological History of the West Indies. 3 Vols. London: Longman, Rees, Orme, Brown, and Greene.

Stevens-Arroyo, Antonio M. 1988 Cave of the Jagua: The Mythological World of the Tainos. Albuquerque: University of New Mexico Press.

Steward, Julian H., ed. 1948 Handbook of South American Indians Volume 3. The Tropical Forest Tribes. Washington, D.C.: Smithsonian Institution Bureau of American Ethnology, Bulletin 143.

Sued Badillo, Jalil. 1978 Los Caribes: Realidad o Fabula. Río Piedras, Puerto Rico: Editorial Antillana.

Sued Badillo, Jalil 1983 Cristóbal Colón y la Esclavitud del Indio en las Antillas. San Juan, Puerto Rico: Fundación Arqueolólogica, Antropológica, Histórica de Puerto Rico.

Tabío, Ernesto, and José M. Guarch 1966 Excavaciones en Arroyo del Palo, Mayari, Cuba. Havana: Departamento de Anthropología, Academia de Ciencias da la República de Cuba.

Tabío, Ernesto E., and Estrella Rey 1966 Prehistoria de Cuba. Havana: Departamento de Anthropología, Academia de Ciencias de Cuba.

Tapía y Rivera, Alejandro, ed. 1945 Biblioteca Histórica de Puerto-Rico que Contiene Varios Documentos de los Siglos XV, XVI, XVII y XVIII Coordinados y Anotados, 2. ed. San Juan de Puerto Rico: Instituto de Literatura Puertorriqueña.

Ullola Hung, J., and R. Valcárel Rojas 1997 Cerámica Tenprana en el Centro del Oriente Cuba. Santo Domingo: Videograph.

Ullola Hung, J., and R. Valcárel Rojas 2002 Las comunidades apropiadoras ceramistas del sureste de Cuba: Un estudio de su cerámica. El Caribe Arqueológico 2:31–40.

Vargas Arenas, Iraida 1990 Arqueología, Ciencia y Sociedad. Caracas, Venezuela: Editorial Abre Brecha.

Vega, Bernardo 1980 Los Cacicazgos de la Hispaniola. Santo Domingo, Dominican Republic: Ediciones de la Museo del Hombre Dominicano.

Veloz Maggiolo, Marcio 1972 Arqueología Prehistorica de Santo Domingo. Singapore: McGraw-Hill.

Veloz Maggiolo, Marcio 1976 Medioambiente y adaptacion humana en la prehistoria de Santo Domingo (vol. 2). Santo Domingo: Universidad Autónoma de Santo Domingo, Coleccion Historia y Sociedad 30.

Veloz Maggiolo, Marcio 1991 Panorama histórico del Caribe precolombino. Santo Domingo: Edícion Banco Central de la República Dominicana.

Veloz Maggiolo, Marcio 1993 La Isla de Santo Domingo Antes de Colón. Santo Domingo: Edición del Banco Central de la República Dominicana.

Veloz Maggiolo, Marcio, Elpidio Ortega, and Mario Sanoja 1976a Preliminary Report on Archaeological Investigations at El Atajadizo, Dominican Republic. Proceedings of the Sixth International Congress for the Study of Pre-Columbian Cultures of the Lesser Antilles: Guadeloupe. Pp. 283–294.

Veloz Maggiolo, Marcio, Elpidio Ortega, and Angel Caba Fuentes 1981 Los Modos de Vida Mellacoides y sus posibles origenes: Un estudio interpretivo. Santo Domingo, R.D.: Museo del Hombre Dominicano.

Veloz Maggiolo, Marcio, I. Vargas, M. Sanoja O., and F. Luna Calderon 1976b Arqueología de Yuma (República Dominicana). Santo Domingo: Taller.

Versteeg, Aad 1987 Saladoid houses and functional areas around them: The Golden Rock site on St. Eustatius (Netherlands Antilles). Paper presented at the 12th Meeting of the International Association for Caribbean Archaeology, Cayenne, French Guiana.

Versteeg, Aad H. 1998 Inhabitations and environment in the Guianas between 10,000 and 1,000 B.P. Paper presented at the Seminaire Atelier Peuplements anciens et actuels des Forets tropicales, 16 octobre 1998. Laboratoire Ermes/Orstom, Orléans, France.

Versteeg, Aad H., and Kees Schinkel 1992 The Archaeology of St. Eustatius: The Golden Rock Site. Oranjestat: St. Eustatius Historical Foundation, Publication No. 2.

Vescelius, Gary S. 1980 A cultural taxonomy for West Indian archaeology. Journal of the Virgin Islands Archaeological Society 10:36–39.

Walker, Jeffery B. 1990 Analysis and replication of lithic materials from the Sugar Factory Pier site, St. Kitts. *In* Proceedings of the Eighth International Congress for the Study of Pre-Columbian Cultures of the Lesser Antilles. Tempe, Arizona: Arizona State Anthropological Research Papers Number 22, pp. 69–79.

Walker, Jeffery B. 1985 A preliminary report on the lithic and osteological remains from the 1980, 1981, and 1982 field seasons at Hacienda Grande (12PSJ7-5). *In* Proceedings of the Tenth International Congress for the Study of Pre-Columbian Cultures of the Lesser Antilles. Pp. 181–224. Université de Montréal: Centre de Recherches Caraïbes.

Walker, Jeffery B. 1993 Stone Collars, Elbow Stones, and Three-Pointers, and the Nature of Taíno Ritual and Myth. Ph.D. Dissertation. Pullman: University of Washington.

Watters, David R. 1994 Archaeology of Trants, Montserrat. Part 1: Field methods and artifact density distributions. Annals of the Carnegie Museum 63:265–295.

Watters, David R., and James B. Petersen 1995 Trants, Montserrat: The 1995 Field Season. *In* Proceedings of the Sixteenth Congress of the International Association for Caribbean Archaeology. Pp. 27–39. Basse Terre: Conseil Régional de la Guadeloupe.

Watters, David R., and James B. Petersen 1999 Is La Hueca style pottery present at Trants? *In* Archaeological Investigations on St. Martin (Lesser Antilles). Corinne L. Hofman and Menno L. P. Hoogland, eds. Pp. 299–301. Leiden, Netherlands: Faculty of Archaeology, Leiden University.

Watters, David R., and Irving Rouse 1989 Environmental diversity and maritime adaptations in the Caribbean area. *In* Early Ceramic Population Lifeways and Adaptive Strategies in the Caribbean. Peter E. Siegel, ed. Pp. 129–144. Oxford: B.A.R. International Series, 506.

Watts, David 1987 The West Indies: Patterns of Development, Culture and Environmental Change since 1492. New York and Cambridge: Cambridge University Press.

Whitehead, Neil L. 1988 Lords of the Tiger Spirit. Dordrecht, The Netherlands: Floris.

Wilbert, Johannes 1996 Mindful of famine: Religious climatology of the Warao Indians. Cambridge, Mass.: Harvard University Press.

Williams, Dennis 1985 Ancient Guyana. Georgetown, Guyana: Ministry of Education, Social Development and Culture.

Wilson, Samuel M. 1990 Hispaniola: Caribbean Chiefdoms in the Age of Columbus. Tuscaloosa: University of Alabama Press.

Wilson, Samuel M. 1993 The cultural mosaic of the indigenous Caribbean. Proceedings of the British Academy 81:37–66.

Wilson, Samuel M. 1997 Surviving European Conquest in the Caribbean. Revista de Arqueología Americana 12:25–40.

Wilson, Samuel M. 1999 The Emperor's Giraffe and Other Stories of Cultures in Contact. Boulder, Colorado: Westview Press.

Wilson, Samuel M. 2001 Cultural pluralism and the emergence of complex society in the Greater Antilles. *In* Proceedings of the Eighteenth International Congress for the Study of Pre-Columbian Cultures of the Lesser Antilles. St. George's, Grenada Vol. II, pp. 7–12.

Wilson, Samuel M. 2005 Stone Pavements, Roads, and Enclosures in Central America and the Caribbean. *In* Proceedings of the Twentyfirst International Congress for the Study of Pre-Columbian Cultures of the Lesser Antilles.

Wilson, Samuel M. 2006 The Prehistory of Nevis, a Small Island in the Lesser Antilles. New Haven: Yale University Publications in Anthropology, No 87.

Wilson, Samuel M., Harry B. Iceland, and Thomas R. Hester 1998 Preceramic connections between Yucatan and the Caribbean. Latin American Antiquity 9(4):342–352.

Wing, Elizabeth S. 1989 Human exploitation of animal resources in the Caribbean. *In* Biogeography of the West Indies. Charles A. Woods, ed. Pp. 137–150. Gainesville: Sandhill Crane Press.

Wing, Elizabeth S., and E. R. Reitz 1982 Prehistoric fishing communities of the Caribbean. Journal of New World Archaeology 5:13–32.

Woods, Charles A. 1989 Biogeography of the West Indies. Gainesville: Sandhill Crane Press.

Woods, Charles A., and Florence E. Sergile 2001 Biogeography of the West Indies. Boca Raton: CRC Press.

Yoffee, Norman 2005 Myths of the Archaic State: Evolution of the Earliest Cities, States and Civilizations. New York: Cambridge University Press.

Zeitlin, Robert N., and Judith F. Zeitlin 1996 The Paleoindian and Archaic Cultures of Mesoamerica. *In* The Cambridge History of the Native Peoples of the Americas. R. E. W. Adams and M. MacLeod, eds. Pp. 45–121. New York and Cambridge: Cambridge University Press.

Zucchi, Alberta 1991 Prehispanic connections between the Orinoco, the Amazon, and the Caribbean area. *In* Proceedings of the Thirteenth International Congress for the Study of Pre-Columbian Cultures of the Lesser Antilles. Curaçao: Reports of the Archaeological and Anthropological Institute of the Netherlands Antilles, No. 9, pp. 202–220.

Zucchi, Alberta 2002 A new model of the northern Arawakan expansion. *In* Comparative Arawakan Histories: Rethinking Language Family and Culture Area in Amazonia. Jonathan D. Hill and Fernando Santos-Granero, eds. Pp. 99–122. Urbana: University of Illinois Press.

Zucchi, Alberta, and Kay Tarble 1984 Los Cedeñoides: Un nuevo grupo prehispanico del Orinoco Medio. Actas Científica Venezolana 35:193–309.

Zucchi, Alberta, Kay Tarble, and Eduardo Vaz 1984 The ceramic sequence and new TL and C-14 dates for the Aguerito Site on the Middle Orinoco, Venezuela. Journal of Field Archaeology 11:155–180.

INDEX